Spiritually and Financially Free

Born to Be *Alive*

By Chris McGrath

10 9 8 7 6 5 4 3 2 1

DEDICATION

To my three sons Christopher, Shane, and Joshua:

Besides God, they make life worth living...

TABLE OF CONTENTS

INTRODUCTION

Are you a believer in God but feel empty when it comes to your relationship with God? Do you see God as uninvolved in your life and in humanity? Or do you see God as careless with you and others, leaving you to start to perhaps question and doubt God's interest in you and your life? And have you felt let down by churches that only seem to be concerned about your attendance, but not about your own personal growth and connection with God? And do you feel a calling to be a better leader as a disciple of Christ?

If you do, then this book is just for you...

This book is about how to become a covenant leader and how to balance your life in all eight areas, namely, spiritual, family, health, business, finance, mental, relationships and lifestyle. I call these eight areas the "wheel of life" because the only way your life is going to ride smoothly is if all areas are strong enough to hold up the weight of these different areas of life. If even one spoke or area of your life is weak, your wheel of life will wobble badly and hinder your life experience. But when all eight areas of your life are firing strong, your engine of life runs smoothly.

Most programs aim to only help you in one or two categories of life, but this one can help you in all of them, if you choose to follow it.

You should be living an abundant life in every category. Living an Abundant life, Jesus promised us, *"I came to give you life and life to the full."* Peter says, *"For you know that it was not with perishable things such as silver or gold that you were redeemed from the empty way of life handed down to you from your ancestors." "You are filled with inexpressible and glorious Joy."* But this does not appear to be seen in Christian living. It appears more like drudgery – no different from what we see in stressed-out non-believers lives who constantly worry about money, their jobs and their future...

Where is the Abundant life for Christians and everyone else too?

Everything in our human experience doesn't just come to us. We must be proactive. However, with God it's different. We must find God and then learn how to communicate, observe God's natural laws and walk with them in faith, in the unseen world.

The physical world is easy to follow. It doesn't take much effort. In the secular world, you don't need to think about your faith, process questions about the deeper meaning of life, think about things like why bad things happen to good people, or why would God allow Hitler to even exist. In that world, we don't go to the effort to strip away the opinions of other people and instead we end up overly concerned about what others think about us. This leads us to living an inauthentic life where we miss the mark of God's teachings of who we should be. In other words, we get caught up in our own egos in a sort of self-righteous way that serves no one.

For example, I have seen leaders who are very dogmatic in their teachings. Early in my career as a preacher, I followed other leaders who were like that. But later, I realized that their style of leadership was not right. Their leadership style was never in the spirit of what Jesus would have intended but mirrored more of the autocratic style of the Sages and Pharisees in the Bible. These dogmatic religious leaders were overly strict with rules and regulations and turned away from the loving guidance from God's Word.

In addition, in this secular world, when life gets difficult and you feel like you are swimming upstream, you don't have to learn patience with others and yourself or be steadfast in your convictions. You don't have to exercise your faith. That is your choice. God gave us the gift of free will.

But if God allows us to be wicked or not, then what is God trying to do? The answer is that He is trying to create love in this world. But he wants us to choose it. And he wants us to look to Him and seek the answers so that we will understand.

This is a book to give you hope that by putting your trust in God and by embracing the teachings of Christ Consciousness that you will find the ultimate joy. The teachings and the principles will lead you to an abundant life. And they apply to every aspect of your life.

I think there is a grave misunderstanding in the Christian world about money, ambition, excelling, and doing your best. I see churches that have programs, events and general messages preached. But the message and the effort are always in accordance with what the preacher thinks is best, which is usually, quite frankly, heavily influenced by the desire to keep their job, and not how to meet the personal needs of the everyday Christian.

I am not down on Churches, as I was a preacher. I see the value in the fellowship and having a community to connect with. But it's limited because the number of members always greatly outranks the number of those preaching and teaching, just like a schoolteacher who can't teach 30 children as well as 10...

I believe that you must go back to the basics and take your relationship with God to the next level.

How?

By continually being authentic, working on your attitude, and by creating your vision of God, your vision of your life, and your character to serve people. Churches have let us down in this regard as there is very little leadership providing solutions to these issues.

The Abundant life requires a deep desire to know God. It involves a search of who God is and how you too, made in the image of God, are a co-creator in your experience that we call life. By searching for this relationship with God, you enhance every aspect of your life. So, is there anything more important in life than finding a relationship with God?

God gives you hints and ideas on how to find him. For instance, you can find him by observing science or by looking at the world and the universe. Or, by observing how the stars are aligned, how planets are perfectly placed, how gravity works, how the moon affects the waves of the ocean, or how the earth is perfectly placed at the right distance from the sun. If we were an inch closer we would burn, or an inch away we would freeze; how amazing is that?

The other way to "find God" is to have faith. The Bible basically says, *"Have Faith, plan your life and watch what happens."* One of the ways to gain and sustain faith is by reading about God from inspired literature, from the Sages and Wise Men of Old. There is a universal intelligence that is helping life on earth. That intelligence is God, manifested in the life of Jesus Christ.

This is a book for people who are searching to know God or for those who have plateaued in their relationship with God, failing to find the Abundant life. What I have found in my own experience in life is that when you include God into every part of your life, everything becomes much easier. From attracting abundance, to attracting the best partner for you, when God is there, what you want manifests so much easier.

What are some other reasons to seek God? A good reason is to answer life's questions! All of us want to know why we are are here, what is the meaning of life, and what is the best way to live it. But also, when you do seek God, you define who you are in the process. Another reason is that who you are becoming equips you to create the Abundant life.

Of course, there are those who believe that God doesn't even exist. Some may wonder, why doesn't God make himself more obvious to help us to know for sure that he exists? I would answer that he makes himself very obvious. Creation itself is proof. Design through function and form of everything from insects to animals, to us, is proof. The proof is extremely obvious when you think about it. There are many natural God-created things on earth that man cannot even come close to duplicate.

I believe that many people don't want to believe in God simply because they don't really want to research it. Jesus spoke in parables. A parable is an earthly story with a heavenly or spiritual lesson. Jesus used them as a filtering system. He said, *"though seeing, they don't see, though hearing, they don't hear."* The point is that the real seekers search. It separates the flaky searchers from the real ones – those who want to know God. No one is interested in a flaky effort to know you. We can sense that immediately when we talk to someone. So can God. Searching is about the heart and the giving of your heart consistently. This is our crucible in life: to know God.

One of the benefits of seeking God is that He totally satisfies the need within human beings. If your need is to feel safe and secure, then God will fulfill that. If you need to create, then God will be a co-creator with you totally satisfying you. If your need is to contemplate man's existence in the science and theology of life, then God will help to guide you to find the answers. God will challenge you, enlighten you and meet every need you have. If your need is adventure, pioneering, or exploring, then God will give you all the frontiers that you need. He will give you the zest for life.

If you want to live a life of peace, God will allow you to dwell in a sanctuary of eternal peace. These are the desires of our hearts. That is why we innately have a thirst to know God. There is a hole in our lives that only God can fill: a resting place for our souls.

I encourage and even implore you to seek him. He is waiting for you and he will make life wonderful and abundant for you in all ways, no matter where you are in your Christian faith.

Matthew 7:7 says, *"Ask and it will be given to you. Seek and you will find. Knock and the door will be open to you."* All you have to do is to ask! The next step is to believe that what you have asked for is going to come to you. But most of us don't believe. Hopefully, this book will help you to get your faith back, and to learn to trust in God so that you can have the abundant life.

Jesus says it with confidence, that if you apply yourself, you will get what you are looking for. He says that there is no doubt that God will respond to you. That is liberating! There are no conditions on that. It doesn't matter what background you come from or what type of personality you have; it is totally unconditional. You can find God at whatever level you desire. You are the measuring stick in your walk with God.

My son Shane was 4 years old when I took him to a store to do some shopping. He wanted to go to the toy section; I needed to shop. So, I tied a big blue balloon to his wrist that stretched way above the aisles in the store. I lead him to the PlayStation area; then I let him play his games. I stood and watched to see if I could see the balloon, from a distance. I could see it clearly. Then I went about my shopping, looking over my shoulder ever so often to see the balloon. When it came time for me to find Shane, I looked for the balloon and with confidence I knew if I followed the balloon, I would find Shane. Sure enough, I found him, and we went home. It was a joyful experience.

That is the confidence that God wants us to have when we are looking for him. Follow the signs that he has left, and we will find him. What a great search in life to have a deep, meaningful, and personal relationship with God. This is God's desire and yours whether you are consciously aware of it or not.

How we relate to God and see God is totally subjective. God has endowed us with unique talents, gifts, and personalities. It is through these gifts and talents we have a paradigm that is unique to us. Through this paradigm, which is personal, we see God. There is no person, no church, and no authority that can define that for us. It is personal. When we believe and embrace that, we find the God we seek and love. When we are true to our original self, we align ourselves through the right portholes to see God.

There is a challenge with this; combating these ideas is Satan, using social conformity, using religion past and present, using leaders of influence, using self-doubt, questioning God, questioning the rights and wrongs of God, and using history and human involvement. This is the maze of life that can either help you or hurt you depending on your humility and trust in God.

This is a book on how to chart your way through this maze of life. I will help you understand your unique endowments – not to apologize for who you are, or to question who you are, but to believe that your presence on this Earth is a gift from God in this mural of human "being," experiencing life.

We will cover 8 principles: 1) Being Authentic, 2) Attitude, 3) Visualization, 4) Enjoying the Process (Character), 5) Biblical Philosophy, 6) The Cross (Love), 7) Leadership with Gratitude and 8) How to prepare your mind for action. These 8 principles will help you in whatever endeavor you take on, whether that be money, family, career, health or relationships in order to attain that abundant life that Jesus promised.

Accompanied with this main book (sold separately) is a subsequent workbook which will give you the necessary nuts and bolts of accomplishing what you want. It will help you to strategize, prioritize your goals, eliminate unnecessary goals, and keep track of where you are. It is a "start any time" weekly/monthly/yearly planner that you can use to become the engine of your own ship to become and remain the captain of your own ship.

So, with confidence, enjoy your search in this maze. God is holding up a big blue balloon to help you find Him...

CHAPTER 1: AUTHENTIC

"An unexamined life is not worth living" – Plato

To create an Abundant life, we must first start with You being authentic: you being true to yourself. You learning to know you. Most of us grow up learning the lesson of getting criticized for being our true, authentic selves. We learn from our parents, siblings, other relatives, classmates, teachers, and those in authority what is considered to be right, wrong, or acceptable...

WHY IT'S HARD TO BE AUTHENTIC

This is why for many of us, being authentic is such a difficult thing to achieve. We have been trained to not think on our own, to only do what is acceptable by other's standards, to not draw outside the lines that are given to us, and to not stick out, shine or excel. This worship of mediocrity, sameness, and the way things are keeps all of us stifled and serves no one. It is diversity, creativity, and authentic self-expression that is not only our calling, but the calling from God that He wants us to honor and respect.

You didn't come here to planet earth in order to become a robot and "be" like everyone else. You came into this world, all bright-eyed-and-bushy-tailed to embrace the very essence of God from the perspective of creating your life, and more importantly, YOU in this magnificent journey of the human experience.

For most of us, this kind of talk about being authentic seems refreshing and invigorating, when all along, it should have been par for the course – it should have been driven into your subconscious mind that you are a piece of God in every sense of the word – a ray of God – made in his image – powerful and creative.

This is why you may be feeling like something is missing in your life. Usually, anyone who picks up a book like this doesn't do so because everything is going right in their lives, but because something feels amiss – something doesn't feel right. That "something" usually is the simple case of not being your true, authentic self, realizing it, and then making the decision to do something about it.

Unfortunately, I see this conformist attitude perpetrated upon the people from the very preachers who are supposed to be assisting you and guiding you towards God's teachings of following your own heart, and being your true, authentic self. As Joseph Campbell so aptly put it, "follow your bliss," but you won't get a whiff of bliss if you don't first become an authentic person.

What are some practical questions to ask yourself to see if you are being authentic in your own life?

Here are some questions for you...

Are you doing work that satisfies YOU, or someone else? Did you truly decide who you wanted to become and what you wanted to do, or did you succumb to outside pressure from others? It's never too late to become your authentic self, but it bears the question, when you were young, did your parents, siblings, friends or other relatives push you into becoming or working in a field that you didn't really like, or was it totally *YOUR* decision, with no outside influence?

So many of us get stuck working in jobs we hate, so we can pay for cars and homes that we can't afford, in order to impress people who don't even really care about us! That is the explanation as to why statistically speaking, 85% of earth's population *DO NOT LIKE THEIR JOBS*.

You may be a lucky one, in the small category of the 15% who likes what you do and perhaps you didn't let anyone push you into doing what they thought you should be doing. But even then, how much of your life is *YOU* being your authentic self? In this situation, the question to ask is, "When do I say yes to people when I want to say no?" When you say "yes" to someone when you want to say "no," is that being authentic? When you say "yes" when you mean "no," you may think that you might hurt the other person by refusing to help, but, you are actually hurting and dishonoring yourself, let alone, being inauthentic...

This isn't to say that being of service to others is not good or important – of course it is. Being in service to others is the foundation of ANY good small or large business, and it's also, of course, needed to help the needy. But if the service that you offer puts yourself in jeopardy of following your own heart and being your true authentic self, then the service you offer is not authentic and hurts you more than helps. Give from a loving, free heart after you have filled up your own cup. When you give from your surplus rather than from what you need, the giving feels wonderful, because it comes from the abundance that you have. But while you are building the foundation of your own life, it's very hard to help others build theirs too.

TAKE CARE OF YOU FIRST

In other words, take care of yourself first, and then the service you give is one that truly feels good. That's called "authentic service," or authentic giving – giving from a happy, cheerful heart.

You must get to a place in life where you don't care anymore what others think about you so that you can be your true, authentic self. "What others think about me is none of my business" say some spiritual teachers. When you get to the point where you don't care what others think about you anymore, which may take a long time to totally embrace, you will *FINALLY* be free from the shackles of other's expectations of you...

If that is where you are now, quite frankly, it's going to be a challenge in order to change. It's hard to start to suddenly say "no" to others when most of your life you have bent over backwards to say "yes." Guilt will first set it. You may start to fear that others will suddenly stop liking you. And to be quite honest about it, they may start to not like you if they aren't the type who you should have in your life anyway.

It is inevitable that whenever you take on a new challenge like becoming more authentic, you're going to ruffle a few feathers, stir up the pot of your life, and not really even know until the dust settles who is your real friend, or not. Most people will understand, especially if you explain to them that you're working to become more authentic.

But honestly, it's awkward to come right out to others and say, "Look, I read this book about becoming spiritually and financially free, and it encouraged me to become authentic. One of the ways to do that is to start standing up for myself more. So, the next time you ask me to do something for you, I may say 'no.'"

Wouldn't it be nice to be that upfront with it? If you feel comfortable, explain it that way, in your own words of course. Those who truly love you will understand. Those who don't, well, then the question is, do you really want them in your life anyway?

One of the things that you learn in life as you get older is that our precious time on planet earth goes by quickly, and if you're not careful, you can end up living it by default – meaning, living your life based upon what other people expect of you rather than you taking the bull by the horns and steering it. Or, as in the analogy of the ship, it would be like going out to sea with no rudder and no sail, just letting the ocean currents of public opinion guide you whimsically to whatever destination others think you should take.

The truth is, however, that if your ship hits rocks and sinks before you even get to shore, will anyone else take full responsibility? Of course not. They will dismiss it and you as you suddenly must re-create yourself anyway.

So many of us get stuck in corporate jobs when in our heart of hearts, we long to be our own boss – we long to create our own companies, businesses, or ventures. But no one is really stuck! You can truly be, do and have whatever you want when you choose to follow your God given heart and let go of those relationships that hold you back.

It takes courage to be yourself! That is really a strange thing to have to say when you think about it. You have to love God and yourself first before others, just as a mother with a child on a plane where the oxygen level has suddenly dropped MUST put on *HER OWN* oxygen mask *BEFORE* her child's mask. The reason the airline stewards stress this so much is because they know that if you don't take care of yourself first, you will be useless to anyone else, including your children.

In other words, you have to take care of yourself before you take care of others.

WHEN IS IT OKAY TO BE "SELFISH?"

Do not believe that you're being selfish by putting yourself first in your endeavor to be authentic. If you succumb to the pressure of putting other people first at your own expense, then isn't it obvious that they are the ones being selfish? Why is it okay for them to be "selfish," but you can't? It's so ironic how others will call someone selfish when what they are really saying is that it's okay for them to be selfish, but not you!

The word "selfish" is simply a word that others use to control you into submitting to what THEY want, which is actually being selfish by their own definition. Stop giving in to the control and set yourself and your soul free from the expectations of others. You deserve it!

Most of us spend so much time worried about what others will think about us that we lose sight of who we really, truly are and our own goals, dreams, and aspirations. So, if someone calls you selfish, just smile and say, "Well, yes, there's some truth to that! I've gone most of my life not focused on what I want, trying to help so many others, and it got me into this precarious situation where I'm not happy. My happiness is especially important to me, and so if me wanting to be happy is your definition of 'being selfish,' then yes, I'm very selfish. But I choose to embrace it for a while until I find my balance!"

Most people think that it's selfish and materialistic to have *money* as a goal – to become well off, or even, dare I say, "rich!" *"Again I tell you, it is easier for a camel to go through the eye of a needle than for someone who is rich to enter the kingdom of God"* says Matthew 19:24. But what the scripture was really trying to say is that if you become greedy and focus all of your life's attention on just making money, your spiritual side, your family side and all of the other sides from the "wheel of life" will suffer. But if you become balanced in ALL aspects of your life, don't be surprised if one day you wake up, realizing that you are now abundant in all areas of your life and rich in comparison to where you were before.

"Rich" is such a subjective word anyway, right? The term "rich" in the Bible could have been meant for the top 1% of the top 1%. If that word doesn't work for you, exchange it with "abundant" or "well off," or "gainfully employed" – whatever feels best to you. When you focus on YOU first, then ALL aspects of your life will improve.

This book is meant to help you to become your true, authentic self so that you can design the life of YOUR dreams, YOUR goals, and YOUR aspirations because it is YOUR life! It's not your spouse's life. It's not your parent's life. It's not your sibling's life. It's not your teacher's life. IT'S YOURS...

ANSWER YOUR OWN QUESTIONS

To become more authentic and to create a more abundant life, I would suggest using the process of "Answering Your Own Questions."

What does answering your own questions mean? Well, there are a lot of opinions out there in the world that have been provided by very smart people and not so smart. How do you distinguish the difference? For instance, there is a lot of information we can get from the internet. Some of that information is well researched, others not. There are libraries full of books with great advice and knowledge on all subjects. However, the authors motives, we don't know. Usually, it's either to brag about what they know, to make money, document their findings to help others, or some combination of these. How do we know? We don't know. Motives are important because it communicates the depth of their research and integrity.

But what about You? What are your passions? Did you ever really take the time to figure it out?

What is Your Passion?

One way to find your passion is to answer the following question...

Let's say that you were given a trillion dollars 5 years ago, and during this time, you traveled to every single place that you wanted, you bought every home and car you ever wanted, and now, you're sitting in your mansion, wondering what to do with your life...

What would you do now?

A similar question was asked of a young man in an audience who wanted to become an engineer. After the teacher asked him this question, his honest answer was, "I don't know." The teacher then said, "Well, I can give that to you right now!" The audience laughed because it was a great point...

The point is that most of us have never given much thought to what we really, really want on a deep level. We spend most of our lives struggling to get by or to "make it" without even considering what it is that we really want. Instead of figuring out who we really are, we allow other's opinions to cloud our own thinking, or we think way too small, inhibiting our true potential.

How would you answer this question? It's really a great way to figure out what you truly want. What would you do if you had already bought everything you ever wanted, traveled every place, and done everything?

What now???

Do you want to know something remarkably interesting? The most satisfying answer to this question always turns out to be the same thing for 99% of us...

And what is that?

"To be my most authentic self possible, follow my heart, be joyful, and to be of service to others..." As it turns out, the Bible really is correct that there is more happiness in giving than receiving.

"But, you said to put yourself first – how is that being authentic?" you may ask...

The answer is, when you finally fill yourself up, your natural inclination is to want to help others. That is what God wants you to discover *ON YOUR OWN*.

What is the point of all this then?

It's to make the point that what you really want is something that you can start doing TODAY – you don't need to wait. Of course, there is absolutely nothing wrong with "being selfish" for a time until you get to the place where you can do what comes so natural to all of us, which is usually to help others. Most of us, made in the image of God, want to help move humanity forward by using our God given talents and skills. It's what brings us the most satisfaction because it feels really good to give to others. There really is more happiness in giving than there is in receiving. This is why many wealthy people give to charities and foundations that they believe in.

But of course, if you're just starting out, your focus should be on mastering your own talent and skills so that later you can help others. With this new understanding of what it is that you will truly want when you get to the end of your goals and dreams, why not give at least a little to others along your journey to "making it?" Why not get yourself into the habit of being in service to others now in small ways to fulfill the true desire that you have within your heart?

Today, teaching others online is a huge business practice that almost anyone with any skill can do to make money. More and more websites are making it easy for people with skills to teach and share.

The point is that inside you is a powerful, spiritual being who wants to bring joy and inspiration to others in whatever way you want – you get to choose. It could be that you want to become a musician, teach others, and inspire through your music. You could be a writer, inspire others through your writing, and then help others to do the same thing. Or, perhaps you want to build a business and then once you've made it, teach others. The possibilities are endless, and since you are a ray of God made in his image, you have talents and skills that the rest of the world will value and appreciate.

It doesn't matter how you choose to be of service to others – it could be completely unrelated to your career in the sense that you could be a volunteer fire-fighter who owns an accounting agency.

Again, it's your life and you get to choose!

The question then becomes, what do you want written on your tombstone, as the late Dr. Wayne Dyer used to say. He also used to say, "Do not die with your music still in you."

What is your music playing in your heart that you want to share with the world? What do you want to be remembered as? Who are you, and what makes you "feel alive?" You were "born to be alive" and share your magnificent self with all of humanity.

THE LIBRARY WITHIN YOU

I believe we have a library within us. When we understand our own passion and convictions, we can then formulate ideas that spring from within us. You are part of God or source energy and you create the course of your own life. How you live your life comes down to your ability to understand the questions that bubble up within you, internalize them, then discipline yourself to act upon them. Questions arise within us all the time!!!

My belief is that our creator is trying to talk to us through these questions and tries to help us create the abundant life. The problem is we don't hear the questions because of all the noise that is going on in our heads. Our real questions are vying for our attention but competing with the "entertainment impulse or the stress and worries of life." These questions arise at a rhythm in your life, through the ups and downs and chaos of life.

How conscious are you of these rhythms and why are these questions percolating? What is happening now in your life? Ask yourself, why am I bubbling up these thoughts? If we look at the great song writers or poets, they write their best material at poignant times in their lives. In other words, when they suffer a great tragedy, they create their best work. They are aware of themselves by identifying their feelings, thoughts, and questions. They ask the deep questions of life and themselves, and then put it to paper to share with and help others who may be going through similar difficulty.

If you are cognizant of your own thoughts, feelings, and emotions, you will write your own life's music or etch your own wisdom in poetry. You will create your own library of life and reference what works for you, what's important to you – not another's opinion, but yours. It depends on how well you know yourself. This is how you become the author of your life.

God gave us our emotions for a reason. He gave them to us in order to help ourselves guide our own lives based upon our source energy connection to God. Through our emotions, we know what feels good and what does not. It's as simple as that.

But what has been battered and knocked out of us is how to listen to our own "inner-being" or that "gut instinct" that God uses to speak to us through his Holy Spirit. When you learn to trust and put your faith in Him, then you will be guided every step of the way in your all-important quest to give more than you receive.

In regard to your intuition, how many times in your life did you make a "mind/head" decision over your "heart," only to discover afterward that you should have gone with your heart? How many times has something gone wrong in your life because you didn't listen to your heart and you said to yourself, "I *KNEW* that was going to happen!"?

Even now as you're reading this, your heart will tell you that this is true. Truth resonates at a higher vibration and you can instantly tap into truth if you pay attention to how it feels. We all have an inner lie detector tester going on if you know how to listen closely to how things feel to you. Your feelings are what God has given you and what God uses to help you to connect to Him and your inner wisdom. You don't have to study the Bible for decades or go meditate under a tree for your whole life – all you have to do is to pay attention to how you feel.

HOW TO KNOW WHAT YOU WANT

Why is it that some people just know what they want? These are confident people who have direction in their life.

I believe it is because they know who they are. They know what they want and what they don't want. They understand what makes them tick, at least in the area they value. When you know who you really are and what you really want, then it is a lot easier to traverse life and make the correct decisions that we all must make on our journey through life.

Have you ever noticed how good, powerful leaders are never fickle? They are decisive. They are authentic. They value themselves and know what they want. They don't second guess themselves. They are not wishy-washy, insecure, or not sure of themselves.

More of us can be that way too of course.

Everything will be tested in time; how a person builds their whole life will be tested. As for you, are you building? If yes, then, what are you building? As you go through life, you will need a radar system to detect your important questions. That system is your conscience, working with your questions, aligning you with your higher values! It will help you evaluate your emotional and spiritual health.

FORTIFYING YOUR FOUNDATION

When the trials come, and they will, will you be ready? Jesus puts it this way; you will either build your house (life) on the rock, or the sand. One will stand, and one will fall. Building your life on the rock is what stands and is the stronger foundation. Jesus says his words are the foundation to build your life upon: being authentic, true to yourself, opening up to feeding your heart and mind, and contemplating values that Jesus spoke about. This is how you connect with your creator or the spiritual world; by answering your own questions, you create a gateway to building a solid foundation leading to an Abundant life.

Life is going to happen to you whether you like it or not. Do you want to have a say in your life? Or do you want to live by default and let others create it for you? Life is lived through YOUR opinions, NOT SOMEONE ELSE'S.

What are your opinions and desires? Desires well up in you and they need attention and direction. What are they saying to you? We have to, or even better, *get* to enjoy the process of guiding our own spirit. God won't impose his will on you, but Satan sure will. Look around at the atrocities of the world. This is Satan imposing his will in our world today.

ASK, AND IT IS GIVEN

But we never have to give in to the temptations from Satan, because as Matt 7: 7 says, *"Ask and it will be given to you."* When you ask, it is given. Through the contrast of your life, or the "bad things" that have happened, you have automatically asked for what you want. The next step is simply to have the faith in God that whatever you ask for will be delivered to you.

The main problem with most of us is that we simply don't believe that it can be so easy – "Ask, and it's just given? Hogwash!" says our subconscious minds. And because we don't believe it, or have faith in it, then we block it from happening. You get what you believe, and if you don't believe, you won't receive...

If God knows how many hairs are on your head, and loves you so much that he knows everything about you, then you have nothing to worry about – your abundance can easily come through...

EXAMINE YOUR WAYS

Jesus expected us to ask God about our concerns or problems but how can we know them, if we don't ask ourselves what they are? Lamentations 3:40 says, *"Let us examine our ways and test them, and let us return to the lord."* Asking our deep, personal questions is imperative to the health and happiness of our lives.

When we recognize negative thoughts and feelings that we have, we are grateful that we can turn away from these thought patterns. In every moment, we have the option to think either a better feeling thought from where we are, or a more negative one. And whichever one you choose has momentum. In other words, if you think a negative thought, entertain the thought for a bit, and then think another negative thought, it's hard to stop the downward spiral. But if you can catch yourself in the first negative thought, you can stop it before it gains any momentum.

The point is that you have the choice to think a more negative or a more positive thought on any subject you think about. When you purposely choose the better feeling thoughts, you naturally progress towards your inner-being thoughts – the thoughts of God.

On Sunday mornings, a lot of churches take communion as an act of remembrance of Jesus. Jesus asks us to do this to remember him and his sacrifice. The cross represents God's humility teaching us how to think a different way – to take responsibility for our thoughts and behavior and aligning them with what God considers a better way to live.

This slow purging is the salvation of our soul. We reflect on our lives the past week. We see our bitterness, slander, gossip, complaining, hatred, lust of people or material things. We learn how unfulfilling these thoughts are and how these were the very same thoughts that murdered Jesus.

But also, these same thoughts are murdering us today. When we allow ourselves to think these negative thoughts, we grow in our understanding of what life is like without Jesus. We get a chance to reflect on how our lives would have been without Jesus. You understand without God's love, life will wear you out; it is chaotic.

If this is a practice that is good once a week, my question is, shouldn't it be daily?

My Life Questions

Here is a list of my own questions. Perhaps you have or had some of them too:

Question #1: When I was 18, I had a lot of questions. My father and mother divorced after 25 years of marriage. This brought a lot of pain to our family. I felt and saw the pain of divorce firsthand; it was horrible. Who do you support? Your mom, or your dad? What a horrible question for a teenager to have to answer. There was so much bitterness on my mom's part with how she felt my dad treated her. My dad didn't know that he was mistreating her. He felt that if she just communicated her feelings, he would have understood.

My dad came from an era where men didn't talk about their feelings. They just grunted and got on with it. This to my dad was an act of love, as strange as that may be. What hurt my dad was his father left him at 11 years old to go and fight in the British army, in World War II. My grandfather was Irish. He left Ireland to go to England, so my father grew up with no father. He didn't know what a husband looked like.

My mother was incensed and unforgiving; she didn't understand him. She decided to divorce him, and this broke my dad's heart. He lost his desire for life. It crushed him and he was never the same after that.

My question was, *why did this have to happen?* How does this happen? Two people love each other starting out in life. They have a family, working the hard years together. Then when the kids leave, they are full of bitterness towards each other just at the point when the golden years are about to start for them. How do lovers get to this place? Is this what marriage is really like?

Question #2: This question came again when I was 18. When I was 17, I was an Irish boxing champion. In the "Irish Times," I read about a person who I had boxed. He served the United Nations Peace Corp Army and was killed in a skirmish while in the Middle East. I couldn't believe it looking at his photo in the newspaper. I thought to myself, "I just boxed you a few months ago and now you're dead?" *How could a young man be killed so carelessly while trying to do good?* In other words, why do "bad things" happen to good people?

Question #3: I tried to understand politics, but I couldn't make sense of it. It seemed that you had to have a deep understanding of any of the topics. Still, even if you did follow it closely, some of the decisions that were made didn't make sense! I started to realize that men have their own agenda that wasn't about the people, but about their own self-interest. Corruption is rampant in politics. When I realized this, that is when I began to ask, *who can you trust to lead?*

Question #4: I grew up in England, then moved to Ireland at 15. Northern Ireland had continual fighting between the IRA and UDA. Every day there was senseless killing in the news. *Why can't we have peace?* This was supposed to be a religious war? What? I thought religion taught love! This wasn't love. Isn't "religious war" an oxymoron? Those two words shouldn't even be in the same phrase. How could a religion approve the killing of others? Didn't Jesus say to *"love your enemy and pray for those who persecute you?"* So, how can it be possible to rationalize the killing of others in the name of religion and God?

Question #5: A major influence in my life at the time was a racist. What is wrong with the color of people's skin? We are different and that should be celebrated, not hated. Something was wrong with this!

What I have also noticed is how the news media tries extremely hard to stir up racist feelings in all of us. They pit us against one another to cause problems in order to drive us apart.

Question #6: Gay rights became an issue, and I didn't know whether that was right or wrong. What was right or wrong if we are all free individuals? Where was the code for right and wrong? What would God say now?

Question #7: A high school sweetheart of mine broke my heart; she had a relationship with one of my best friends. It devastated me. *Where was the loyalty?* I had so many questions in life. In my observation, life seemed like a conveyor belt that you step on when you were born and then the journey through life began with its up and downs. You commit yourself to people and they either bring you joy, or pain. Then you're dropped off the conveyor belt, dead! *Was this really life?*

The other question that came up to me in contemplating this was, how can I stop allowing others to control how I feel? As I got older, I got a little wiser about this and realized that it no longer served me to allow outside circumstances, people, places, or things to get me down. It's simply not worth it.

Question #8: Life seemed so meaningless – meaningless, meaningless. Life made no sense to me at all. I kept thinking, *isn't there more to life than just this?* That was my question. But when I asked people about life, there were so many different opinions! Who was right? Who could I trust? What could I trust and what could guide me? What wisdom has stood the test of time over several generations? These questions lead me to search for the meaning of life...

THE CORRELATION BETWEEN WAR AND SELF SABOTAGE

I don't know where you are in your journey or whether you believe in God or not but here are some thoughts for you to consider:

Humans have suffered more at the hands of each other than through natural disasters.

At the end of the century, the number of people who died a violent death at the hand of their fellow human would rise to more than one hundred million. They died not only through wars between nations, but also through mass exterminations and genocide, such as the murder of twenty million "class enemies, spies, and traitors" in the Soviet Union under Stalin. Then, of course, there were the unspeakable horrors of the Holocaust in Nazi Germany. They also died in countless small internal conflicts, such as the Spanish civil war or during the Khmer Rouge Regime in Cambodia when a quarter of that country's population was murdered.

These were questions that triggered me. *What is it about human nature that makes us want to destroy each other?* Is it really just our fellow human beings who want this? Or is it our corrupt political leaders and rulers?

In thinking about all these deep questions, it's a good idea to start to ask yourself some questions too. If we are quick to want to wage war with other humans for whatever reason, is it possible to turn our thoughts and feelings against ourselves too?

WORTHINESS AND SELF SABOTAGE

This line of thought brings up the question, what is it about *Your* nature that perhaps sabotages You? Many of us have a feeling of not being worthy which is almost always something that we have been taught since we were born. Our educational system teaches us very early that if you don't learn X, Y and Z, then you are not good enough. It is even taken to the level of grading us where our worthiness is displayed for us and everyone else to see in the form of letter grades from A to F...

When we believe that we are not worthy, then whenever we strive to accomplish anything, we risk our subconscious mind silently having its way with us in the form of self-sabotage.

But you can overcome negative thoughts and beliefs in order to live the life that you truly want, without having to live it by default – in other words, the way others think or want you to live it.

Life is going to happen to you whether you like it or not; so, don't you want a say in it? Don't you want to live your life the way you want to? The way you choose?

Right now, you may be asking yourself the question, "But wait a second... Isn't it selfish and a sin to think that I should live my life the way that I want to?"

THE TRUE DEFINITION OF SIN

The human condition is due to original sin, but the term sin has been largely misinterpreted or misunderstood. In the ancient Greek, which the new testament was written, to sin means to miss the mark, just as an archer who misses the target. So, to sin means to miss the point of human existence. It means to live unskillfully, blindly, and thus to suffer and cause suffering. Again, the term, stripped of its cultural baggage and misinterpretations, points to the dysfunction inherent in the human condition. We miss the appropriate response to many situations.

In other words, since sin is really about missing the point of human existence, and the point of human existence is to embrace the creative, god-like being who you really are, then of course it's not a sin to live life the way that you want to.

You were born connected to God. It is more "sinful" to dis-own your own wants, desires, and goals than it is to "fall-in-line" with the wants and desires of others, whomever they may be...

WHAT QUESTIONS DO YOU HAVE?

The questions above and many more were the questions I had in life.

When all these questions arose, I didn't know what to do with them. I had to sort out what was important now and what could be left on the back burner.

But I knew that the questions that I needed answering now would rise like cream that would come to the top – meaning, if you keep reading and talking, the main issue will appear again and again until you could identify the one that resonated with you – the one that comes into harmony with what you feel. (I know that "feeling" at times can't be trusted because they are associated with many cultural factors. But I am assuming that you want to know God and are coming from a good space. Your journey will help you to distinguish what is a trustworthy feeling or not.)

I talked to people who had some experience in this field, and every answer people had I played the devil's advocate. This would lead me to certain knowledge on the question that I needed to be answered.

Then it would come down to my choice on the matter. This is when trusting my gut became significant. I didn't know it at the time that I was developing my own infrastructure – my own value system that would serve me for life. Even writing this book is crystallizing my thoughts about life, philosophy, and theology. Through this, I could see my body, mind, and spirit as a conduit to answering my questions in life. What it showed me was that I am the source of internalizing these thoughts and deliberately creating my pathway through life. What a reassuring value to gain! I began to know me and my own way of figuring things out.

What helps me is to write my questions down and I'm sure that it would help you too. Now, whenever I am not clear, I just write about what I am feeling. You can do the same thing. And when the right question is asked, you will say "That's what I am asking."

THE COURAGE TO BE YOURSELF

Try to stay authentic. This is hard because most of us have become so overly concerned about what others think about us, that we are terrified to speak our own truth – to be real – to have the courage to be ourselves. It's also hard because it is so much easier to have someone else figure you out and tell you the way. We get so overly trained in our school system to answer questions like a robotic monkey without any freedom of thought that we think that we must approach everything in life like that. It takes courage to stand up for yourself and to have the clarity of mind as to who you really are and what you truly want.

But as you get older and wiser, which is the natural progression of most humans, it will become easier and easier to be your true, authentic self. But I am simply asking, why wait?!

Why not do it now? Why waste more time of your life living the life that someone else has designed for you?

THE COURAGE TO ASK TOUGH QUESTIONS

Some of the questions that need to be asked may be a bit painful and you may not like what you hear coming from God or your own inner-being thoughts. But it's only painful in the sense of feeling regret for not living the life you were meant to live. And regret, like the feeling of worry, is another useless emotion that doesn't do any-thing but help you stay stuck and to wallow around in the mire of self-pity. It's unnecessary. Let go of who you have been and focus on who you want to be.

Innocence seems bliss, but it's not. Being spoon fed keeps you a baby emotionally. The joy of life is embrac-ing all of it – everything from the contrasting "bad things" to the wonderful, blissful things and understanding that it's all part of life. The "bad things" that happen to you are simply the experiences that you have that you think are bad, but in the long run, are the very things that help to define who you are and what you want.

THE VALUE OF CONTRAST

It is through the contrast of your life that you become much clearer as to what you DO want. Contrast shows you what you don't want so that you will know what you DO want. Therefore, contrast is valuable. When you look at life through the lens of valuing ALL of it, then you will have no regrets. And when you have no regrets, you can be more authentic and learn to live more in the here and now instead of the regretful past.

Without contrast, there would be no photograph. Without the "bad things," there is no creative energy for the opposite, nor expansion of your soul. This isn't to say that you must endure pain in order to gain. Emotional pain is much more of a choice than most of us realize.

You can take two people who have the exact same negative experience, and one could come out of it fine, and the other be devastated by it. What's the difference?

Perception and choice...

One could perceive the event to not be that big of a deal, and the other could perceive that it's the most devastating thing that has ever happened to them. One will choose to think the most positive thought that they can from where they are, and the other will quickly spiral down into a negative abyss of devastating thoughts and feelings.

Same event. Two different perceptions. Two different choices of thought...

Your true authentic self is strong, powerful, and connected to source or God. Your true authentic self knows that God is always there to call upon, and never loses faith. Your true, authentic self values YOU and would never entertain disparaging words about yourself.

That's who you really are. One of the secrets to life is understanding that the "lows" that you have happen to all of us, and let you know that you are alive. Just as with life, your heartbeat on a monitor is up and down. When it flat lines, you're dead!

Life is up and down and the trick to all of it is to enjoy the journey of life whether it is up, or down. Enjoying the process is the value of becoming something you aspire too; it is not the goal that is the value. It is who you have become during the process and answering your own questions that serves this. In other words, you didn't come here to reach one goal or even a certain number of goals and then die either a success or a failure. You came here to enjoy the journey – to enjoy life to the fullest. That is what God wants for you. The goals or dreams that you have are just the excuse for you to have the joyful journey!

Pay attention to the questions that are bubbling up within you, take them seriously, and God will start to answer them for you.

Chapter 2: Down, but Not Out

"All I can control is myself and just keeping a positive attitude" – Rose Namajunas

I was an Irish boxing champion. I had a huge fight, in a place called Galway, Ireland. It was 1979 and I was representing Ireland against England. The rivalry between England and Ireland goes back generations. The Irish hates the English because of the way they treated them in the past. The Irish felt like the redheaded stepchild. The English looked down on the Irish, as peasants.

The atmosphere in the audience was intense. I was scheduled to fight a guy named Ruben Christie. The bouts preceding my fight, I was sitting amongst the crowd watching them when this guy behind me, who was very large in size and who had a strong West Indian accent, was shouting and screaming support for his English colleagues. When he was yelling "Kill them! Destroy

47

them!" it struck me, and the people sitting around me, that this guy was taking it a little too far.

I got into the ring and was introduced as the Irish representative. Then, along with his entourage, my opponent came into the ring with a hooded gown, looking like the grim reaper. As his name was announced, he pulled his hood down and much to my surprise, it was the same guy who minutes before was yelling "Kill them! Destroy them!"

I nearly jumped out of the ring and ran home! (I am glad to say, I didn't do that.) At this point of my boxing career, I never lost a fight. This was going to be a challenging night tonight, I thought to myself.

We met in the center of the ring, where the referee spoke to us. We had the intimating stare going on. The bell sounded and we came out for the 1st round. My strategy was in all fights to land the first punch. That usually was a left Jab. In most cases that would happen and rock my opponent back on his heels. From there it was an uphill battle for them. But tonight, it was a different case!! I threw my first punch but like in the movie "The Matrix" when the agents fired bullets at Keanu Reeves, he could see them coming, swivel out the way then "destroy them." Well, Ruben Christie could do that too. He saw my punch coming, swiveled to the side and unleashed a heavy punch. At that moment, I remembered the words "Destroy Them! Kill them!" when I was in the crowd. My inner voice said, "We are going to be destroyed tonight, maybe killed."

I am happy to say that did not happen. However, I knew this was going to be a different fight. I was in for the fight of my life.

The 1st round was tough, but I would say a draw. The 2nd round became a surreal moment in my life. Boxing is about setting your opponent up for the big punch or punches and looking for your opponent's weaknesses. Then, when that moment arrives, you move in for the kill. Ruben Christie set me up, then landed a punch that knocked me down. It was surreal because when I was down on the canvas, which was very rare, the crowd was shouting at me to get up – so was my coach, family, friends but not my girlfriend, of course. She was yelling, "Stay down honey, he's hurting you!"

In hindsight, it was surreal because I had to face the facts. I was the only one who could decide to get up and continue the fight. I was down but I wasn't out of the fight. I needed to decide what was I going to do. Should I stay down? Or Get up? If I got up, with what attitude? Attitude is everything in life.

In the game of life, we are fighting for what we believe in and want in life. However, we can become broken down by circumstances, by finances, by divorce, by corporate re-structuring, by children in trouble or addictions in our own lives. This may knock us down in life. Something like this may have already happened with you. The question now is, how have you responded?

THE THREE RESPONSES TO LIFE

Before we discuss the three responses to life, it's important to understand that in order to even have ANY response to life at all, you must first "put yourself out there." You must be playing in the game of life. In other words, *having any one of these responses is better than not ever having anything to respond to at all.* Stated another way, what is even worse than trying and failing is never trying at all because of fear.

The Fear of Failure

At least in this first response to life, you have decided to enter the ring – to play in the game of life. Many people don't even get in the ring or play on the field of life. But if you give up before you even try, that's actually worse than failing. The rational thinking in our subconscious mind is that not even trying is better than the possibility of failing. After all, if you don't even try, how can you fail? And if you don't fail, no one can point out any failure that you've ever had. The logic goes that if you don't even try, then you will never fail!

But we do ourselves and others a huge disservice in life with this attitude of not even trying, and many of us suffer from an unfounded fear of failure – a fear that paralyzes us into never even living.

Think about it...

When a baby first starts to learn to walk and they take their first step and fall, technically, they failed. They could have thought before trying to walk, "Well, that walking thing looks difficult. I think I'll just crawl around here on the ground for the rest of my life! After all, I've got my mom and dad here to take care of me, and there are too many scary things that can happen if I learn how to walk! What if I fall and really hurt myself? Or, what if I fall and someone laughs at me? That running thing is even worse – that looks way too dangerous!"

A baby never thinks this way. They intuitively understand that failure is part of the process. They know and have faith that eventually, they'll get it. They don't beat themselves up with negative self-talk about how disappointing it is that they can't walk yet and they don't think thoughts like, "Is there something wrong with me?" Regarding what others think, they could care less. Why? Partly because they haven't been brainwashed into caring more about what others think about them than what they think, and also because they don't have any concept of failing as being bad. But also, because they intuitively know that being able to walk has many benefits!

What happens to us as we get older? When did we start to begin to worry so much about what other people think about us? You may think this doesn't apply to you, but there is probably something that you decided to not even try because of what other people might think. Take, for example, public speaking. Or, singing. How many of us can sing but we don't even really try because we get embarrassed by what others think? I used to be that way.

Founded Vs. Unfounded Fears

Fear can be categorized as healthy or unhealthy and unfounded. An example of a healthy fear is the fear of a grizzly bear. Your natural fear of petting a wild grizzly bear even though it may look cute and cuddly keeps you from being eaten. That's a good fear to have! But an unhealthy, unfounded fear is fearing something that is not dangerous at all, you know it's not dangerous, but you still fear it. Another example of this would be claustrophobia or the fear of public speaking.

It's important to understand these types of fears before we get into the three responses to life because if you let unfounded fears rule your life, you'll never even get out there onto the playing field of life. When you decide to be a spectator in life and never get on the playing field, you will end up being disappointed with yourself when you're on your death bed. I don't mean to be so blunt about it – I'm just telling you like it is so that you never get to the point in your life where you regret not trying things that you really wanted to try.

In chapter 8, we will discuss tools and techniques that you can use to get over limiting beliefs and any fear of failure that you have so that you can start on the wonderful path of failing. I say it this way to lessen the negative connotation that you may have about "failure." When you develop a better attitude about failing, and when you can see it as part of the process, then so many more options in life become available to you.

Now, let's talk about the 3 responses after being knocked down in life...

The *first response* after suffering a blow in life is to stay down. Give up. Stay defeated and never try again. This response happens when we are not prepared for "the blow" that happened to us, along with the lack of ability to handle the situation, plus a lack of faith and belief in ourselves and in God. With this first response, the first time you suffer a hard blow, you just give up. Many people who start up a new business do this. As soon as they hit a problem, they give up and move on to another whiz-bang business idea that they will also probably drop once it gets hard. Most businesses fail within the first 5 years because of this first response.

This **second response** option is to "get up" after being knocked down but get up with a bad attitude. In my case, I could have gotten up thinking, "I'm doomed to die; why did I ever decide to even fight? This guy's gonna kill me! What was I thinking? I should never have done this!" You could blame others for your predicament, get mad, sad, or even depressed. It is a valiant decision to get up, but when you do it with a bad attitude, you make it many times more difficult to succeed...

The **third response** is to get up with a positive, curious heart – a determination and resolve in your heart to fight your battle and win...

Just to be clear, sometimes, if you KNOW you're in over your head, it's best to quit, go back to the drawing board as they say, or the training, and build yourself up so that you can fight another day. But usually, most of us are not in a life-or-death situation, and we do have it within us to succeed, but we just lack the self-confidence and the gumption to progress – to move forward in our dreams – to fight on. This is what I am trying to help you with.

Let's have a look at each response to "getting knocked down" in life either metaphorically or literally more closely.

After the life-blow first happens, acknowledge that it happened. Tell yourself that it's okay and that you're going to survive it. Most of us do.

In the **first response** option, you feel hurt, annoyed and your energy has been drained. What's this choice? Stay down – stay under the radar – life is too painful. Why get back up into life's fight? It only brings pain! I don't want that anymore. I don't care about my dreams and aspirations anymore. I'd rather not even try than to try but then fail. So, give up! Go through the motions of life just surviving – living paycheck to paycheck, for example...

In many ways, my dad did this. He was raised without a father. At the age of eleven he was responsible to feed 6 siblings. His mother put the burden on him to hunt, fish and to feed the family, which he did! That was way too much responsibility for an eleven-year-old! Then when my dad met my mother, he didn't have much ambition. He associated that with taking on extra burdens, which he didn't want to feel. I believe he was stunted in growth, as a boy, by being given too much responsibility. He was burdened too young. Ambition had a correlation with pain to him. So, my dad chose to stay under the radar of life – to avoid feeling pain.

Is this where you are? Avoiding pain? Running from circumstances in your life? Not being your authentic self? Is this really how you want to live? Do you feel like it's better to not go after your dreams because you don't want to endure the emotional pain?

If yes, consider that failure really is the price that you pay for success. The question to ask yourself is, when I'm on my deathbed and all is said and done, will I regret not even trying to go after my dreams? What will it be like to be at the end of my life knowing I should have gone for it? That maybe I could have succeeded?

You can do something about this. This is the first response.

In the **second response** scenario, life gives you a hard blow. You're down because someone got promoted and you didn't, for example. You feel cheated out of something in life. You get up, but with a bad attitude. You tell yourself that life isn't fair. You give up integrity because you don't see it in anyone else anymore. Your attitude becomes that people are going to pay for what happened to you in life! Basically, you are angry and bitter at life because it isn't turning out the way that you thought it should. You look for someone or something to blame and you find them! They did this to you and they're now going to pay for it. You're stuck in victim-hood...

This person is filled with bitterness, rage and anger. The energy they give off is, "I am not happy." They have an ax to grind. They are miserable in life and they let everybody know it.

Sadly, I had a cousin named Greg who was overcome with bitterness and anger. As a boy of 13 he would join his 15-year-old sister, Anna, after school, and they would walk to their grandparents home to help with chores. They were encouraged by their parents to do this.

His sister always seemed reluctant, but she obeyed her parents. My grandfather would take them to the "bog." This was the name they gave a field where you dug "Moss Pete." My grandfather would send Greg out to cut the turf while he took Anna into a shed and had sex with her. Greg had no idea that this was going on. This went on for some time. A few years later, when Anna got married, she couldn't consummate her marriage (Gee, I wonder why!). As she was seeing a doctor about this, my mother asked her, "Anna, has grandfather violated you?" My mother said, "Don't be frightened to talk about it; he did it to me!"

Then everything came out. It was a horrible discovery. It left Greg feeling guilty and mad that he couldn't defend his sister. He cursed my grandfather out. When my grandfather died, he urinated on his grave. He became so enraged and bitter, that one night, while driving, he was going too fast and hit a bridge – a bridge he was familiar with. It flipped his car into the river, and he drowned. There was no alcohol involved. The bitterness ate him up every day. I am not saying that his anger towards his grandfather caused the accident, but it sure didn't help.

If you don't take responsibility for your attitude, your pride will take you for a ride. It will lead you into places you never thought you could go. Even if you feel justified for your anger, it's not worth it. All of us must find a way to forgive others or forgive ourselves so that we don't allow anger to eat us up alive from the inside out. Stress and anger are known to create more stress hormones in the body like cortisol, which have been proven to make cells more susceptible to acquiring cancer and to suppress the digestion and immune systems.

It's simply not worth it...

Own your attitude. Don't give your power away to some irrational thought pattern. When you let others control how you feel, you give them the control and power over your life and your emotions. Why would you do that? Anger, resentment, and other negative feelings like that are not from God...

Do you find yourself getting triggered easily? Do you have fits of rage? Are you critical of others or of everything? Do you never have a good word to say? Does being kind and nice feel fake to you? Do you feel like this isn't the real world?

You can change this too... This is the second response.

In the **third response**, life delivers you a heavy blow. You are crushed. Maybe it was a divorce you didn't see coming. Maybe you were fired from your job for no reason. Or you lost your house. You are angry, upset, feeling this isn't right or fair but you realize this isn't a state that you want to remain in.

These feelings are unhealthy, *BUT* you have a strong feeling this isn't you. You know that this is just a temporary feeling, and that with enough work on yourself, you can get yourself into a better feeling place.

The pain and the circumstance are real but they don't define your life. They don't define you. You know that you can overcome it and you work to purposely think better feeling thoughts. "I am nothing special," they tell themselves; "this happens to everyone." This type of person takes control of their thoughts and emotions instead of letting thoughts and emotions control them...

What separates people is how they deal with it. How you deal with it is your choice. You can choose beforehand to deal with a heavy blow from a place of faith, empowerment, and confidence, or not. It's really up to you...

Another cousin of mine was raised in West London. I'll call him Harry. His older brother was Tom. Tom and I were close, but I hardly knew Harry. Their parents unfortunately were victims of the disease of alcoholism. Tom had told me on many occasions that he would come home from school and find his parents lying in the street, drunk.

His parents separated. Their dad, my uncle, was found dead in his apartment, 2 days after his death...

Harry, the cousin who I didn't know very well, had many challenges in his life. I remember meeting him with Tom when he was 16 years old. He really struck me as someone who wouldn't be held back by his circumstances. He met his High School sweetheart and they married very young. Sadly, she passed away after only 2 years of marriage. Then Tom, his older brother, dropped dead at a bar. He was inflicted with the same disease as his parents.

Harry's parents couldn't put him through school. He found a way to do that for himself. With all the difficulties he faced in life, he never gave up believing something good would come out of his life. At the death of his wife, he was empathizing with a business client of his, about his client's life. When the client found out what was happening in Harry's life, this client was so impressed with his attitude during these difficult times, that he asked Harry to work for him. They were one of the richest families in London. Harry became a top surveyor in London.

Today, Harry is happily married with 2 children and a beautiful wife. He owns a lot of property. His company was the most sought-after acquisitions company in Europe. Amid all the tragedies of his life, he never stopped believing he could do something with his life. Now, he is a multi-millionaire living a purposeful life. He created a scholarship for actors, in honor of his brother Tom who was an actor.

He went into politics to help people. He has had an audience with The Queen and Tony Blair. His wife and children are blessed by his fortitude.

Everything has to do with attitude. If you faced the same circumstances, would you have persevered? This is the Third response to life knocking you down. I say that these types of people get back up with a "curious heart" because they are resolved; they chart their own waters in life. They take total responsibility for their attitude regardless of the circumstances. They recognize the reality of life, however, they're curious of how to overcome life's challenges. They want to know the strategies, the healing tools of life. They are not scared to look at themselves and see who they really are.

Going to therapy, reading, talking, observing, examining human behavior, or trying to understand pain; this interests them. It isn't taxing to them in their journey of life. Again, that is one of the secrets to life – to understand that the blows you experience are nothing more than a part of life – something to learn and grow from.

Dave Asprey became a millionaire at 26 but wasn't satisfied about his health and the educational information on food. He discovered how the marketing world hides the truth from us to serve their own financial gains. So, he spent millions of dollars figuring this out. He lost over 100 pounds in weight and created a term call "biohacking" that is now used in mainstream language. Biohacking is about hacking the truth about biochemistry as it relates to your health. His company "Bulletproof" is dedicated to helping you in your health. He does it through book writing, podcasts and emails. He has made many great discoveries about health. He didn't need to do that. He could have basked in the sun doing nothing. But he had a "curious heart" about life and he knew that he could help others.

Dr. Joel Furhmen was an Olympic skater but had a terrible accident that injured his ankle. He was told to have an operation, but he chose not to because he believed his body could heal itself, which, he did. His dad owned a very successful shoe store in New York city, and he was set up to be wealthy. Joel's dad wanted him to become business partners, but Joel chose to become a doctor on health and nutrition and how the body can heal itself. Again, this is a great example of the "curious heart" that has a different attitude in life.

There are many more examples to show us that there is a different way to responding to the knocking down of life.

So, this begs the question, how have you shown up in the challenges of life? When you are knocked down, how do you respond?

Do you stay down under the radar of life? Or do you get up with passive/aggressive anger and become destructive in your contribution of life? Or are you curious in searching for the answers? Are you a curious student of the study of life?

It takes courage to suffer a blow, decide to get back up on your feet, and choose to have a positive outlook and a "curious heart" about life. It's not easy. Emotionally, it can be hard at first because it forces you to face the truth. But in another way, it's much easier because once you train yourself to see the light at the end of the tunnel, or the glass as half full instead of half empty, you can get yourself into a spiral UP, instead of down. You can talk to yourself as if you are your own life coach, giving you encouragement and strength. And of course, you can also find that courage and strength through God's word and your faith in Him.

The truth is that with these three types of responses to getting knocked down in life, you must deal with emotional pain. Since you're going to experience emotional pain no matter which of the 3 responses you choose in all three scenarios, why not choose the one that gives you the best results? Why not choose the one that empowers you rather than gets you down?

Negative thinking is a much more destructive thing than most of us realize. It is what destroys people more than anything else in life. This is why you can tell the difference between and angry old person and one who is not. You can actually see the results of years of negative thinking on the face of an older person. This is why it's your attitude that counts most...

Regarding the emotional pain we are discussing here, you may ask, doesn't everyone feel pain? The answer is, yes. We all do. It's normal. It's called being human. But the amount of pain you hold on to and the length of time that you have it is your choice.

Leaders do not allow themselves to go down a negative thought pattern because they know how dangerous and how bad it can be.

STAY POSITIVE NO MATTER WHAT

One self-help, personal development coach discussed his lunch meeting with a Chinese businessman who is a great example on how to think when things go wrong...

The coach and the businessman had ordered their meal, and so the coach asked the businessman how it was going. The businessman was very wealthy and owned several huge factories in China.

His answer was something like, "actually, things are really bad. Production is way down. Our supply chain is broken, and sales are the worst they've been in 10 years..."

Then, as the meal was being brought to them, the wealthy businessman nonchalantly said, "but it's okay. Things always work out. Can I get some water please?"

He barely even acknowledged the "bad things" that were going on in his business and powerfully chose to focus only on the good – that things always work out one way or another.

This is a great example of how you and I can be when things aren't going well. You can admit the truth, *BUT LEAVE EVERY TOPIC ON A HIGH NOTE OF POSITIVITY*.

That businessman knew that everything would work out somehow. He probably had been through the process many times before, and that is why he spoke about it so confidently. But experience doesn't really matter. If you and I can have the same positive attitude, and leave EVERY topic in our lives on a positive note, then things WILL always work out...

THE HIDDEN SPIRITUAL BATTLE

There is a spiritual battle going on whether you are consciously aware of it or not. There are forces that are breaking us, the family, and the fabric of society down. These forces are real, with real people behind them with real hidden nefarious intentions. Many of them are part of the 1% that they talk about, and as time goes on, more and more of them are being exposed for who they really are.

If that is difficult for you to accept, then this may be a hard book for you to read. I am coming from a space that totally believes this. My philosophical positions are built upon the Bible – not on Religiosity – and not what I see in churches today – not on rigid rules, but on the abundant grace of God expressed through the Cross.

A question you may ask yourself is, "Why put your trust in Jesus' words?" My answer is: They have stood the test of time. He is the only one that has risen from the dead.

Without pain, there is no search for God. You don't see your need for him. And when you search for God and find him, the rewards are far beyond what you can imagine.

What level of pain you go through and the sufferings you have are directly related to the philosophies of your life and the decisions you have made based upon these principles. If you believe that life is hard and difficult, then you will have a hard and difficult time when life gives you a heavy blow. But if you believe that there is value in pain and suffering, you can see it as a very temporary thing, greatly reduce its impact, and get right back on track in your life as if nothing even happened.

Be that businessman who quickly turned something negative into something positive. Have that kind of faith in God that He will help you, and then He will help you. It simply never pays to wallow around in the mire of negativity.

But there really is a battle of good and evil in our world today. How you view life, what and who you listen to unconsciously in your life, builds the life that you are living. Both worlds are being attacked which are the religious world and the Secular World. In the Religious world there is a lot of dogma, misinterpretation, judgment, condemning and peer pressure that stops you identifying with the authentic self. In the Secular World there are lots of misconceptions about Christianity, the Cross, and the Church. There is naïveté along with carelessness and a dismissive attitude of weighty evidence about science and personal experiences of life. This attitude hinders healthy principles to build your life upon.

THE SPIRITUAL BATTLE WITHIN YOURSELF

Finding the Abundant life involves you being aware of the spiritual battle going on, not only in the nonphysical realm, but also, within yourself.

Each of us has a spiritual battle going on within ourselves from the perspective of not believing and trusting in God, nor ourselves. Our own negative self-talk, our limiting beliefs, and our negative subconscious beliefs all work against us. It's such an ironic thing that for most of us, our biggest problem is the conflict that we have within ourselves. While one part of us wants abundance and a successful, vibrant life on every level, our subconscious mind wants us to remain small – to not stick out – to be safe and to not take any risks.

When you decide to purposely not allow anyone nor anything outside of yourself to get you down or to start thinking negative thoughts, and when you take total responsibility for your philosophies in life, THEN you have mastered the art of living the abundant life. THEN more and more good things will come to you. THEN relationships will be better and easier. THEN money will flow to you in abundance. And THEN you will have a closer relationship with God, which will reward you in every way possible.

And then when you get hit with a heavy blow from life, you may be down, but you are not out. With the third response, you can achieve your goals and aspirations for your life. With the other options, you unnecessarily suffer.

Now the question becomes, which way do you choose? When life deals you a blow, will you choose to stand up, value the contrasting experience, have a good attitude anyway, and forge forward knowing that God is on your side and helps those who have faith in him? Or, when you get knocked down, will you not even try to get back up, or get up with a negative attitude and sabotage the rest of your life?

It really is your choice and my hope for you is that you choose option 3...

This chapter is meant to help you to be aware of the spiritual energies that unconsciously influence you in the decisions that you make for your life. It's also meant to help to encourage you to choose option 3 when life knocks you down.

In the fight with Rubin Christie, I was down, but not out. I had to decide whether I was going to get up and continue fighting. I also had to decide if I was going to fight with a curious heart, or an already defeated one. So much of life is a choice. When you have faith and belief in God and in yourself, amazing things can and will happen. In my fight, I had to take responsibility for allowing Christie to hit me and hurt me.

After Christie knocked me down, I did decide to get up. I thought to myself, I didn't see that punch coming but it was a good one. I recognized the strategy of how he did it and I resolved he wouldn't do it again.

Rather than let the knockdown defeat me, I decided that whether I won or lost, I had to give it my best shot. It was a calculated decision that I had to make in an instant. Had I not trained hard for this fight, it may have been wiser to not get up. But I had trained hard. I was ready. My curious heart resolved to figure out how to win the fight even though Ruben was better than most boxers.

As I got up before the count to 10, I smiled back at Ruben, calmly acknowledging the knock down. Now, I was galvanized to take matters into my own hands...

Just like in real life, by making those little corrections in how I approached the fight, the fight ended early in the 3rd round with the Green, White and Gold Flag of Ireland being raised victoriously.

But even if I had lost the fight, I still would have felt much better taking that third response option than the other two.

Use this for your own life. Don't ever let life get you down. Failure is the price we pay for success. I really think that failure should be taken out of our vocabulary because it's such a negative, drastic word – it conjures up images of the first response option where you get knocked down and you don't even try to get up...

When you see the blows in your life or the "failures" in your life as *PART OF THE PROCESS* instead of the END RESULT, then you can so much more easily steer your ship in the direction that you want to go – or stated better, become the engine for your ship and powerfully go in the direction of your choice.

FAMOUS PEOPLE WHO NEVER GAVE UP

There are many examples of people who have failed and then succeeded. Albert Einstein didn't speak until he was four years old. Imagine the fear in his mother's heart that he was intellectually challenged! When he was 16, he took the entrance exam to get into the Swiss Federal Polytechnic school and failed it. He then decided all he could do was to become an insurance salesman, but he failed at that too....

Imagine if Einstein had chosen response option 1 and gave up. What if he had allowed his failures to get the best of him?

Dr. Seuss got into Lincoln College, Oxford, but failed and dropped out. He then wrote his first children's book "And to Think I Saw it on Mulberry Street," but it was rejected 28 times. Life knocked him down over and over, but he kept getting up with a curious heart. Today, his books still make enough money for all his descendants to never have to work another day in their lives. According to the Washington Post, by 2015, Dr. Seuss' books had been translated into 17 languages and had sold 650 million copies in 95 countries. His books still make it onto the best-selling lists.

And then, there was Henry Ford. He was a huge believer in the power of the mind when he is famously quoted as saying, "If you think you can do a thing or think you can't do a thing, you're right." But he too failed many times. His first company went bankrupt and his second one failed too. If he had given up, he would never have become successful.

Jim Carrey grew up in an extremely poor family and when he was 15, had to work as a janitor in order to help the family make ends meet. During his first performance at a comedy club in Toronto, he was booed off the stage.

Undeterred, he tried again and again. When he started to make it, he wrote himself a check for 10 million dollars and post-dated it into the future. He kept that check in his pocket so long that it started to wear out. But almost to the exact day of the check, he received a check for 10 million dollars for his role in "Dumb and Dumber."

You may have heard of the book "Rich Dad Poor Dad" by best-selling author Robert T. Kiyosaki. Did you know that he didn't write that book until he was 50 years old? Not only that, but when he was 30, his first business went bankrupt. And then his next one too! If he had given up, he would have never become the success he is today.

You may still think that you don't have the mind of an Einstein, or the talent of a Jim Carrey, or the business wits of Henry Ford. But at first, all of them failed! And they didn't just sort of fail, or kind of fail. They all failed miserably. The point is that the only real difference between you and them is the determination and the willingness to keep on trying. That's all. There isn't some mystical reason. "Genius is 1% talent and 99% percent hard work" according to Einstein. When you are determined enough, believe in yourself enough, and fail over and over again but still get back up, then you can accomplish anything. Just like I said, attitude is everything.

It is really the fear of failure that holds so many of us back. Once you understand this clearly, it will be easier to work towards your goals and dreams. That's the whole point of harping on all of this – to help you to build up the self-confidence that you will need to set your goals and attain them.

As I stated earlier, it is really the fault of our educational system who brainwashes us into believing that failing is a horrible, bad thing and that you are only successful if you can get straight "A"s. That judgmental system causes us to be hypersensitive to failure. That attitude about it keeps us from even trying because of the inordinate fear of failure that many of us have.

If life knocks you down, it never means that you are out. "Failure" is really an educational experience – that's how you learn. One computer programmer teacher of a friend of mine said that he wanted his students to fail when coding because that's how you learn. If you were successful with every line of code, you'd never learn what didn't work!

You are never down and out unless you choose to be. Failure is the actual process of progressing towards your goals and dreams. And when you choose to get back up with a positive, curious heart, coupled with a fiery belief that God is on your side and will help you, then you can accomplish *ANYTHING*.

Chapter 3: Visualize

"Imagination is more important than knowledge. For knowledge is limited, whereas imagination embraces the entire world, stimulating progress, giving birth to evolution." – Albert Einstein

I have a few questions for you that I'd like you to really think about...

When you visualize or imagine in your mind your ideal life, what do you think about? What do you see? Do you find it difficult to visualize because you think you're just not good at it? For some of us, it's easy, and for others, it's not. The question then becomes, how do you visualize? What is the best way to do it? When is the best time? How often should you do it?

Also, what are the tools and techniques that we can use to visualize better?

SPIRITUALLY AND FINANCIALLY FREE

We will cover this topic and others in this chapter in order to help you to visualize what it is that you truly want and how to tie that into your goals. We will also discuss how sports psychologists from Russia can help us to visualize, what kind of results you can expect, how often you should visualize and what is the best way to get it to work quickly. (Hint: emotion is key). We will also discuss the difference between receiving a vision and transmitting a vision.

MADE IN THE IMAGE OF GOD

You are both the receiver and the transmitter of visions. Since you were made in the image of God, you can create whatever vision you want. God gave all of us the gift of free will. And we all can visualize because it is an integral part of memory. If you have a problem visualizing, just think of it as memory instead. How do you remember anything? How do you remember what a red apple looks like, feels like and tastes like if you think you cannot visualize? How do you know if it's fresh or not without the memory and visual of what is stored in your brain: the taste, the smell and the texture in order to tell if it is a good apple, or a rotten one?

You may think, perhaps, that you are not the type to visualize – that somehow, you never received that gift. But if you answer the question of "What is the color of your car?" or, "What is the color of the front door of your house?", you must use visualization in order to get the answer. Or, if you have to remember where you put your keys, you have to use the power of your visualization. If you think of a friend or a relative, you have to use your visualization in order to remember.

Visualization is memory. Anyone can do it. So, you can visualize. You are created in the image of God, so of course you can.

It's the same experience for anyone creating anything.

If you think it's hard for you to visualize, what you probably mean is that it is hard for you to visualize your perfect life – perhaps it is hard for you to see yourself living the life that you really want, having what you want and doing what you want because you don't believe it's possible. The reason why this may be the case has much more to do with your belief in yourself and what is possible for you instead of your ability to visualize.

All of us can visualize. It's just that most of us don't use it proactively or correctly in order to make our dreams and goals come true.

THE VISUALIZATION PROBLEM

Many of us have a problem with visualizing what we want because we don't BELIEVE that we can have what we really, truly want. So many of us have been programmed to believe that we are not worthy of the things we want because we aren't good enough. Not feeling worthy is one of the deepest, most common problems that we all face.

Not Feeling Worthy

Why is it that most of us don't feel worthy?

As stated earlier, our educational system and society in general has trained us nearly since infancy to get us to believe that we must prove ourselves worthy, and that *THEY* are the ones who get to judge whether we are worthy or "good enough." The result is that most of us end up reaching certain "acceptable" levels of success and give up any childhood dreams that we had.

For most of us, we end up pursuing jobs and careers for all the wrong reasons – either because it's what our parents, friends and family wanted or expected us to do, or because we think that we can't make enough money doing what we love. In addition, most of us care way too much about what others think about us with the result being that we end up living lives of in-authenticity which we already covered.

Inner Conflict

The result is that a person can have conflicting inner dialogue going on where others opinions about what you SHOULD want is conflicting with what YOU want. A quite common factor for most of us is that we have pre-programmed parental tapes stored in our subconscious minds that play whenever we go against any of the so-called "rules" that we have created for ourselves. For example, if your father told you when you were little that you would never amount to anything, then that parental tape could play any time you decide to push yourself into "amounting to anything." These subconscious beliefs are huge hurtles that we must jump over if we are going to create the life that we want.

Limiting Beliefs

The ironic thing is that our own subconscious minds, whose focus is mainly survival, is the main culprit that creates our own limiting beliefs. Our subconscious mind stores events from the past and uses them in order to make sense of the world – and where we fit in. This is why an event that took place when we were just a child, if coupled with enough emotion, can be used for us, or against us. For example, if we had a loving family who fully supported us and believed in us, then past events and the subsequent created beliefs would serve us. However, if we had a not-so-loving family that didn't believe in us, past memories and events that we had with them *could* store negative thoughts and feelings about ourselves.

From the circumstances and events that we experienced as a child, we create our reality – which includes thoughts, feelings, and beliefs about ourselves. It is these beliefs that we create that can hinder us our entire lives if they are not addressed.

Your personality also plays a huge role in this. If you had a family that didn't support and love you enough, but you were a rebel, then you can create beliefs about yourself that actually support yourself despite the environment that you were raised in.

Removing the negative emotional intensity behind events from the past is one solution to remove limiting beliefs. We will discuss a couple different techniques and tools that you can use to get past limiting beliefs in chapter 8.

ALL IT TAKES IS FAITH

Jesus emotionally and powerfully said at Matthew 17:20 that "Because you have so little faith. Truly I tell you, if you have faith as small as a mustard seed, you can say to this mountain, 'Move from here to there,' and it will move. Nothing will be impossible for you." Of course, this is hyperbole and an exaggeration, but his point is well-made. When you believe in God, believe in Jesus, and believe in yourself, nothing will be impossible for you. It is only your thinking that makes it so or not. It's straight from the Bible!

From a practical standpoint, if you have trouble visualizing your big goals, one solution is to visualize "interim" goals that will take you to your main goal. The tricky thing with visualizing is that no one can really tell you what works best – you'll have to experiment with it. The key is to use your emotions to determine what feels best or not. Let how you feel help guide you.

THOUGHT AND FEELING

Another main point about visualizing is that researchers and scientists like Dr. Joe Dispenza, researcher, lecturer, author, and corporate consultant, now know that it is marrying the power of your emotions with your thoughts that works best to manifest whatever you want more quickly. In other words, thoughts and visions of what you want coupled with the actual feeling of already having it is key.

Another key is to *FEEL GOOD* while you are visualizing. If it doesn't feel good, change what you visualize. It should feel good to you. And when you visualize, do it for the feeling. Enjoy the process. According to Neville Goddard and Dr. Wayne Dyer, it is feeling as if you already have what you want that will help guide your subconscious mind to help you to create it.

What this means is that once you set up the habit of visualizing what you want, your subconscious mind will start to work without you even realizing it on creatively finding ways and methods to bring your vision to fruition. Once you program your subconscious mind with what you want, your subconscious mind will work 24/7 to create your vision as your new reality.

But you cannot create a new reality from the same mind that created the one that you are in right now. In other words, in order to create your new personal reality, you need to create your new personality first. "Change the way you look at things, and the things you look at change," the late Dr. Wayne Dyer, author and speaker used to say.

So much of our life is created from the perception that we have about it. And when you decide to take the control of your thoughts and feelings rather than allow outside circumstances, events, and triggers to dictate how you feel, then you have mastered the ability to create your reality.

According to Dr. Dispenza, scientific brain research proves that your subconscious mind doesn't know the difference between what you imagine and what you actually experience. Yes, your imagination is that powerful – it can really help you to create the life that you really want *if* you believe that it is possible.

WHAT YOU REALLY WANT

Let me ask you a question...

Why do you want what you want? Why do you want to make a difference in the world, or why do you want to attract more abundance, a better social life or the perfect soul mate? Isn't the reason because you know that when you have those things or the right people in your life that you will *feel better*?

So, if the reason why we want what we want is because it will make us feel better, but the way to manifest it into our lives is by feeling like it's already here (belief), then why not really focus on the feeling? Why not purposely feel great or even fantastic right now regardless of what your current reality is? If that's how you create your reality, then why wait?!

It's really all about belief. Do you believe it is possible? Again, if you have the faith the size of a mustard seed, ALL your dreams are not only possible, but already manifested. All you must do is to belief in it.

The point is that you have the power *NOW* to feel good no matter what your circumstances are. This is how you develop the ability to enjoy the journey of life, instead of looking to some "outside of you" object or material thing to fulfill you.

WHY IT'S OKAY TO HAVE MONEY

If you struggle to see yourself as abundant, you may have a misunderstanding of the scriptures.

Many churches have taught in the past that wanting what you want is bad and even sinful. They quote scriptures like 1 Timothy 6:10 where it says that money is the root of all evil. But if money was the root of all evil, why do so many churches ask for it? Why do they pass around a plate, asking for money?

However, the scripture doesn't say that "money is the root of all evil." What it says is that "the *LOVE* of money is the root of all evil." There is a huge difference.

So, if you're having trouble visualizing what you want, could it be that you have an internal conflict with what you think is allowed or reasonable, versus what you really want? Is it wrong to want to be rich? Is it wrong to have millions of dollars or more? What is the "allowed" amount of money per year that is "acceptable?" Is one million a year too much? Does that make $999,999 per year perfectly acceptable and okay?

The point is that money is not the root of all evil. It is not evil. Much good can be created when you have money. You can help others in many ways, donate to charities, and even employee people if you create a successful business. Even whenever you buy something nice you are helping to circulate abundance to others who work for the company who you bought from.

Let's take, for example, your dream car. You may think that it's not spiritual to want such a materialistic thing. It's bad. You're being materialistic. What will others think? But when you think about it, what is a car, but just metal, rubber, and paint? And if you want a nice one, isn't it true that the higher the price that you pay, the more money employees and other people make who made the vehicle which they can then use to feed their families? When you look at it from that perspective, the more money that you can spend into the economy, the more people you benefit!

Does that help you to feel better about what you want? It should. You shouldn't ever deny what it is that you truly want in life.

Of course, balance is the key to everything in life, and intention.

So, if you have a problem visualizing what you want, ask yourself, why? Why can't you visualize it?

Some people think that the problem is that they just aren't the visualizing type. But that's not true. As we already covered, memory requires visualization. All of us can do it.

What can you do if you struggle to visualize what you want?

THE POWER OF YOUR WORD

John 1: 1 says, *"In the beginning was the Word. And the Word was with God. And the Word was God."* Logic has it that if in the beginning was the "Word," the Word was with God and the Word was God, AND we are made in his image, then our thoughts, our "Word" to ourselves and to others is especially important – whether it be silently to ourselves or out loud to others.

We all know that positive affirmations and saying positive things to ourselves is helpful, and that saying discouraging words to ourselves is very harmful. We don't need scientific studies to prove that to ourselves – it's obvious.

But for most of us, we are not at all careful with our own internal speech – our own dialogue. It is said that each of us have about 65,000 thoughts per day, and that most of these thoughts are not positive! If most of our thoughts are not positive, is it any wonder that many of us struggle to attain our goals and the dreams that we set out for ourselves?

The relationship between our word and our vision is that our word is what sets the vision into motion – it is the "next action step" after visualizing what it is that we want. They go hand in hand and are both necessary steps in order to attain our goals and dreams.

The power of Vision through the imagination can free our lives in so many ways. There is so much development in NLP (Neuro Linguistic Programming) on how the mind and imagination work powerfully together. We see tremendous results for athletes, business development, and therapy. In addition, there is a relatively new healing tool called Emotional Freedom Techniques (EFT) which has been proven by the American Medical Association to work for people who suffer from PTSD. The reason why it works so well is that it can take past traumatic experiences a person has had and basically remove all the negative emotional intensity, usually permanently. In addition to it's efficacy for PTSD, it can also help people to reprogram their subconscious mind by reframing negative events from the past. We will discuss more on NLP and EFT in chapter 8.

God has been working with his people using visualization and dreams since time began. It isn't some new-age phenomenon that has been magically discovered – rather, it is something that God has been talking about through his word the Bible for millennia.

Throughout the Old Testament and New Testament, God spoke to his people through dreams, thoughts, and vision.

However, in secular society, the imagination is shunned upon today as childish, naïve, and cartoonish... If you were ever caught in the classroom daydreaming, you might think that visualizing and imagining things is not a good thing, when the exact opposite is true. It is known that Albert Einstein got into trouble for daydreaming in class and he was one of the greatest inventors of all time!

In my own experience, I have found that there is great value in visualizing. When you get an idea or vision and follow it through, it leads to amazing results. When you think about it, everything starts with imagination and visualization first. When an architect creates the plans for a dream home, imagination and visualization is the first step. When you think of what you want, you use imagination and visualization. When you think of the future, you use visualization. We do it all the time...

MY EXPERIENCE

Let me tell you about my experience...

I was a minister of a large church in London. The church was about 2,000 in number. I was invited to a luncheon church service, in Liverpool St, Downtown, London, by another church group. In attendance was about 400 men – some in bowler hats, some were civil servants.

The meeting for lunch church service was inspiring. And while I was there, I got a thought and vision in my imagination. I thought, we could do this same thing at my church and do it in an awesome way. We had nothing for professional people in our church, yet 4 million people traveled every day into one square mile of Downtown London. What was bubbling up in my mind was to develop a spiritual influence in this city. I thought to myself, "This is the perfect place." It had a fraternity of leadership men and women.

To influence anything, you need leadership. And when you think about it, visualization and imagination is a core activity for any leader. To lead, you have to create a vision of what is wanted, preferred or better than what is. A leader will envision a future, circumstance, event, or condition that is better for those who he or she leads.

In other words, if you are going to lead anyone anywhere, you must have a vision of what the preferred future looks like. Imagine if Martin Luther King couldn't visualize and didn't have "a dream." Would anyone have listened to him at all if he didn't have the dream that one day, all races, creeds and religions would be treated equally? What did he envision when he had that thought? What picture did he paint in his own mind when he thought of what life would be like to be treated equally?

He probably imagined people of all colors getting along, being treated equally, and respecting one another regardless of race. In his mind's eyes, he may have removed the "all white" buses with mixed buses and saw how much better the world would be if everyone could simply be treated as equals.

All leaders must envision what it is that they want — including scientists, inventors, businessmen, businesswomen, or even children. Imagine if Einstein wasn't able to visualize or use his imagination. He wouldn't have been able to invent anything!

Visualization is part of the co-creative process and we all can use it.

IS DESIRE BAD?

There are some religions and cultures that teach that desire is a bad thing – that when you want anything, it is coming from the ego. The idea is that once you have gotten rid of desiring anything, that you will then be more spiritual.

I agree that to an extent, that is true, but the problem is that desire is a very natural, normal thing for any of us to have. The baby desires milk from her mother when she gets thirsty. The same baby desires to walk, talk, sing, dance, and play. You cannot squelch desire. Is the baby bad because of her desire?

The point is that *EVEN THE DESIRE TO NOT DESIRE IS A DESIRE!* That's how normal and natural it is to desire.

It is not bad. What is bad is when negative, nefarious intentions are attached to desire, such as the desire to do harm to others, to control, or to oppress.

VISUALIZATION USES

Visualization isn't just used to create new things – it can also be used in sports. Basketball coach Phil Jackson was considered to be the Zen master of NBA basketball coaches and led the Chicago Bulls and Los Angeles Lakers to many championships.

What he trained his players to do was to take the time to quiet their minds, close their eyes and visualize themselves for at least a few minutes playing perfect basketball. They would imagine every shot going in or playing perfect defense. The result was that Phil Jackson won 11 NBA titles as a coach – a record in the NBA.

In addition, visualization was a huge part of the 1976 Olympics "scandal" for the Russians whose sports psychologists had mastered it. But they didn't want to reveal their secret. After winning way more gold medals than they normally did, the whole world accused them of cheating.

Everyone thought that they had cheated by taking drugs, but all of them tested clean. People were so certain that they had cheated, that they started to claim that they must have come up with a way to test negative when, in reality, they were positive. Finally, under the tremendous pressure to explain themselves, the Russians fessed up.

What was their big secret?

Visualization, of course.

Their weightlifters, ski champions, toboggan athletes and many others used it to excel way past their normal abilities. The most astonishing thing was that visualization even helped the weightlifters. They did this by closing their eyes before a dead lift and taking a few minutes to visualize lifting whatever amount of weight it was that was on the bar. One of the key features was that they engaged every single sense they had – taste, smell, touch, sound and sight. When the athlete finally had done it long enough to fully imagine lifting whatever weight they were about to attempt, they were able to lift much more than normal.

But in my case where I had visualized, where was I getting these thoughts from? Who was giving me a vision? It was so vivid. Was this just me feeling happy, daydreaming? Or was Satan playing a trick on me to swell my ego? Was this only normal thinking stuff?

VISIONS FROM GOD

I believe it was God speaking to me and that I was the receiver of these messages. I think that we receive messages and guidance from God all the time. God speaks to us through our emotions, and we can get intuitive "hits" or information or a "gut instinct" on what to do or not do. When you learn to trust in God for this communication, it becomes clearer and clearer over time, to the point where there is no doubt when you are in tune to God, and when you are not.

I will get into more of the details of how God works with your mind and imagination later, and also how Jesus opens you up to your dreams and desires. A simple test I use at moments like this is: Is this vision hurting, stealing or destroying anything? (John 10:10) Or is it about helping, loving, and servicing others? Does the message feel good (from my faulty thinking), or does it feel good (from God)?

The vision to have people meet at my church for lunch felt like the latter. It's the feeling of the opposite of the nature of the enemy which is to kill, steal and destroy. It's pretty easy to tell the difference between a message that comes from God versus one from Satan! Any message from God feels good, empowering, up lifting and inspiring. Any message from Satan feels like everything but that!

As I started to focus and work on this concept, amazing things started to happen. We started to hold weekly events at the London Stock Exchange, the Crusades, the church building, right in the heart of the legal district of London. Lawyers, Barristers, Bank managers, investment Brokers all started joining us.

As I was focused on leadership, I observed the common denominator of males were rugby players and that a lot of these men played rugby in their High School and College years. Now, they were leaders in the city of London.

Then I thought we should start our own rugby team in order to build a relationship with them and create a core base of leadership. We called ourselves the "Lionharts." We ended up taking 25 guys on a world tour. We played in South Africa and Australia. These countries in the years following returned the gesture by coming to London to play.

What an Abundant life evolved out of that vision! This gave birth to the "London City Ministry."

Let's look at Abraham, Father of the Jewish world. He was 100 years old; his wife Sarah was 75 years old. Up to this point, Sarah was barren and could not give Abraham a child. God spoke to Abraham and changed his name from Abram to Abraham. Which means "A father of many nations." God told Abraham, *"You will have a Son with Sarah and call him Isaac."* He believed God and it was credited to him as righteous. Righteous means right living with God. God made a covenant with him of circumcision. That day Abraham circumcised himself. Where did that notion and idea come from? How did Abraham see it or hold it? Did he imagine it? I say that yes, he imagined it and trusted in God. He demonstrated that trust and connection with God that day by circumcising himself. Pwhhh! He got a vision like I did about London. But thank God it didn't involve circumcision for me and the people in "The London City Ministry!"

Paul addresses this in Romans 4: 17. *"As it is written, I've made you a father of many nations. He is our father in the sight of God, in whom he believed. The God who gives life to the dead and call things that are not as though they were."*

Let's have a look at a few things Paul teaches from this passage. He teaches that God raises people from the dead, plus, God manifests concepts and ideas that he plants in people. (Having said that, people have a part to play in manifesting what God has planted in their heart according to their desires. That's co-working with God.) Paul credits God for raising people from the dead. Some speculate that in Acts 14:19 that Paul was dead. God raised him. God raised Jesus, Lazarus and Tabitha from the dead. Also, that God materializes things that haven't happened yet...

HOW GOD USED THOUGHT AND IMAGINATION

How does he do that? Could it be through thought and imagination? Abraham had his son Isaac who had 12 sons, creating the nation of Israel. Through this nation Israel, Jesus came and gave birth to the Christian world today. There are 2.2 billion believers in Jesus today, not counting the people since Abraham who have passed away. Plus, Abraham is the father of the Islamic nation to which there are 1.6 billion people who look to Abraham as their spiritual father. I would dare to say that God is honoring his covenant with Abraham through thought and imagination.

Throughout the Old Testament, God communicated with his people through their imagination – through their dreams – this is how God would speak to his people. Today that is shunned upon. People back then believed it; today, people don't believe that. We have shut God out. This is what Paul is addressing in 2 Cor 3 regarding the veil over people's minds.

If we are to benefit from the same kind of experiential and dynamic relationship with the Lord that God's people in scripture enjoyed, we must, through the spirit, cultivate the spiritual capacity for an inner life that they possessed. The apostle Paul speaks of this inner life – the spirit-inspired capacity to see and hear spiritual things, as well as the benefits that come with it:

2 Corinthians 3:17-18 says, *"Now the Lord is the spirit, where the Spirit of the Lord is, there is freedom. And all of us, with unveiled faces, seeing the glory of the*

Lord as though reflected in a mirror, are being trans-formed into the same image from one degree of glory to another; for this comes from the Lord, the spirit."

It is the spirit-inspired "seeing" of Jesus, Paul said, that changes our being. As we see his glory, we are transformed into his likeness from one degree of glory to another. This, in essence, is how the fruit of the spirit is produced in our lives. When we cease from striving in our own efforts and yield to the Holy Spirit, and when our faith ceases to be merely intellectual and rather becomes experiential and concrete, our lives begin to reflect Christ's image. As we behold the glory of the Lord, we're transformed into that glory. It is what we see, not how hard we strive, that determines what we become.

In this passage, Paul talks about "mirroring" – other translations say "beholding." The question is, where is the mirroring or beholding taking place? From what we've seen in the old testament, it was in the mind!

Paul led into his teaching about the need to behold the glory of the Lord by contrasting it with the glory of God that was veiled in the old testament. The Jews could not tolerate the glory of God radiating from the face of Moses, so Moses had to cover himself with the veil (2 Cor 3:7; cf. Exod 34: 29-35). Paul found in this an analogy for all unbelief.

Speaking of the unbelieving Jews in his own day, Paul said,

"But their minds were hardened. Indeed, to this very day, which they hear the reading of the old covenant,

the same veil is still there, since only in Christ is it set aside. Indeed, to this very day whenever Moses is read, a veil lies over their minds' but when one turns to the Lord, the veil is removed."

2 Cor 3:14-16 emphasis added and paraphrased says *"The mind of the unbelievers are hardened, and thus a veil lies over them that keeps them from seeing (in the minds) the glory of God. When we turn to Christ, however, the veil is removed so we can see (in our minds) the glory of God. It is this imaginative seeing that transforms us 'from one degree of glory to another.'"* (2 Cor 3:18)

The theme continues several verses later as Paul again discussed the inability of the unbelievers to see the Lord as believers do. He wrote, *"the god of this world has **blinded** the **minds** of unbelievers, to keep them from **seeing the light** of the gospel of the glory of Christ, who is the image of God"* (2 Cor 4:4, emphasis added). By contrast, God has removed the veil over the minds of believers and caused the light to shine into their hearts so they can see the light of the knowledge of the glory of God in the face of Jesus Christ (2 Cor 4:6).

Clearly, the ability to see what believers have and what unbelievers lack is a seeing in the mind. The image of God, the face of Jesus Christ, enlightens the one but not the other. The glory of the Lord is reflected in the mind of one but not in the other. The mind of the believer can be controlled by the Spirit (Romans 8:6) and the eyes of (his or her) heart can be enlightened (Eph 1:18).

But the imagination of the unbelievers is under a demonic stronghold that stands up *"against the knowledge of God"* (2 Cor 10:5). Not wanting to acknowledge God, their imagination became darkened, impervious to the divine light. (Isa 65:2, Rom 1:18-28, cf. Gen 6:5). The mind is sinful, nonspiritual, and always set on earthly things. Garrett Green is surely on the mark when he says, *"Sin can be accurately described as bad imagination."* He adds, *"the sinner... while retaining the ability to imagine, has forfeited the basis on which to imagine God."*

In the context of 2 Cor 3:18-4:4, then, it is clear that what the Lord can cause to pass through the mind distinguishes the spiritual seeing of believers from that of unbelievers. The place where the Spirit produces a reflection of the glory of God in the face of Jesus Christ, is in the regenerate minds of the believer.

Here is where the abstract truth about God's love and glory is made CONCRETE and personalized into a transforming experience in the spirit-inspired imagination of the believer. It is through this spiritual, mental vision that we are transformed by the renewing of our minds (Rom 12:2) and set free from the pattern of this world.

While all believers have this capacity, however, we don't necessarily use it. Though we all regenerate and have a new nature, we still struggle to take every thought captive to obey Christ (2 Cor 10:5). We yet have aspects of our mind veiled and thus experience ourselves as though we were not all God says we are in Christ. Our tendency to trust in our own efforts to bring about transformation as well as our dismissal of the imagination as a central vehicle for giving us access to spiritual realities strongly play into this ongoing veiling of our minds.

We need to recover our sense of dependency on the Spirit of God rather than our own efforts and recover the use of the imagination in our relationship with God to experience the transformation of which Paul spoke. We need to learn how to fix our eyes on Jesus and set our minds on things that are above if we are to break free from the pattern of this world and be transformed into the likeness of Christ (Col 3:2-3, Heb 12:1-2).

This is the 3rd step to creating an Abundant life and Co-Working with God. Again, they are: 1) Being Authentic, 2) Attitude and 3) Vision. Using your imagination and working from the creative world within you is the next step to creating the Abundant life.

How to Visualize

No one can tell you how to visualize best for you because we are all quite different. If you think you have trouble visualizing, then try imagining instead. It's nearly the same thing but doesn't focus so much on forcing yourself to create an actual picture in your head.

Some of us are better visualizers than others. What works for one person, may not work for another. This is why it's best to experiment with different ways of doing it for yourself and then see what works best.

Before we get into the actual steps, there are three things you can do...

Set Clear Intentions

Before you start visualizing, get clear as to what it is that you want. When you say to yourself, "I want to be rich," or, "I want to be healthy," the problem is that the intention is so general and vague that your subconscious mind doesn't have any concrete goal to reach – it's not clear what you really want. It's all very subjective.

But when you say, "I want to make $10,000 per month in both passive and active income from my business and investments," then you're getting more specific.

Also, when you set a clear intention, write it down. There is something about writing down your intentions and goals that seems to give it more power and strength. It's almost as if the written word has some kind of a Godly power to it.

Elevate Your Emotions

If you want to give more power to your intention and for when you visualize, add the emotion of excitement, passion, and determination to it. Talk about it often – get excited about it. Focus on what you want and never or rarely talk about where you are right now.

When you use the power of your emotions along with thought, you can create the reality that you want much quicker.

Practice Repetition

One self-help teacher said that if you write down your goals once a day, you'll become a millionaire. If you write them twice a day, you'll become a billionaire. Just as with anything, the more you practice, the better you become at it. And the better you become at it, the more momentum you will gain. And with more momentum, it will be easier to become excited and feel good without having to "fake it til you make it." You can create a "snowball effect" that will really serve you.

Practice makes perfect.

Usually, it is best to visualize in the morning before you start your day. But you can also do it during the day, and/or in the evening – whatever feels best to you.

Expert Visualization Advice

What many experts now agree on is that it is best to visualize in first person. What this means is that instead of "seeing yourself" in the vision from an audience perspective, instead, see it from your own eyes. In other words, see your hands and body from the viewpoint you have right now. This tricks your subconscious mind into thinking that it's real.

Another key point to visualizing successfully is to engage all your senses. The Russian sport's psychologists discovered that when their athletes engaged all their senses, when they were able to see, hear, smell, touch and even taste the scene as clearly as possible, then it worked the best.

For example, the weightlifters clearly imagined what the room would look like where they would compete. They would even go to the actual place of where they were going to compete so that they could get a clear picture of it. Then, before they picked up the Olympic weight, they would imagine putting chalk on their hands, and feel the sensation of touching and smelling the chalk. Next, they saw themselves walking to where the weight was, grabbing the bar, and then successfully and easily lifting the weight.

It's a little bit different when you are envisioning your ideal life, but we can use the same concepts.

Step 1: Setup Your Environment

You don't really need a special environment to visualize. Think of children who get caught at school daydreaming like Einstein did when he was a kid. You can tune anything or anyone out and start to visualize. But ideally, it's best to do it in a quiet place where you won't be disturbed for about 5 minutes.

In a quiet room, draw the blinds, sit in a comfortable chair and focus on your breathing.

Step 2: Relax and Focus on Your Breathing

Breathe in slowly for a count of 6, and out for a count 6. Do this 3 times. Breathing slowly sends a signal to your parasympathetic nervous system to relax. It's communication to your subconscious mind that you are not in fight or flight mode – that all is well.

Step 3: Visualize Your Ideal Scene – 1st Person

Now, from your 1st person perspective, visualize your ideal scene that would prove to you that you've "made it" or have successfully attained your dreams and goals.

Who is there? What do you see? How do you feel? Really visualize it so clearly that it feels real to you right now.

For example, if you were to visualize your dream house, see yourself as living in it, and enjoying it with all your 5 senses.

You could visualize yourself walking around your huge kitchen which has your favorite meal cooking before your guests who are friends and family arrive. Then, see yourself walking to your front door, opening it up for your guests, and see them walking in looking all around your dream house with eyes of wonder and surprise. Feel their touch as you hug each one of them as they enter. Invite them into your large, beautiful living room where you have your favorite couches and paintings there for them to enjoy.

Smell the smells, hear the sounds, and even taste the food you serve your guests. Really get into the feeling of it so clearly that is seems so real to you that you don't want to leave the vision. You could even have conversations with your guests, show them the backyard, or give them a tour of the whole house.

You can do the same thing with your dream car, or with your dream business. Or you could envision traveling to your favorite country in perfect weather and see yourself there too.

When you get the hang of this, what happens is that you will start to reprogram your subconscious mind in such a way that it believes that what you are envisioning is reality – it won't be able to tell the difference. And then the scenes that you visualize will have a much greater chance of coming into your actual experience.

Focus is key. The more you focus on what you want, the better. Stop thinking about the things you don't want, and instead, focus on what you do.

Another key to this is that when you get good at it, you'll start to want to visualize just for the pleasure and feel-good emotions of the visualization itself. In other words, it will start to feel so good to you that it almost won't matter if it comes true or not! Plus, the better you get at it, the more likely you will be to develop the good habit of visualization.

But what if it doesn't feel good to you? What if when you try to visualize your perfect, ideal life, you can't get past the fact that it feels fake and not real?

Stretch, But Not Too Far

The answer is to set your vision or your goal out there far enough that when you make it, it feels good, and yet not so far out there that it seems unbelievable to you. If your goal is to become a millionaire but it's hard to believe AND you don't have $100,000 in the bank yet, then set your goal to $100,000. Or, if you want to make enough per month to make a million dollars, but you're not making enough yet to make $100,000 a year, set your goal to make $10,000 a month.

You can always increase the amount that you want to make once you make one of your interim goals.

The problem for a lot of us with goal setting is that we set the bar too high and then lose all motivation and inspiration when we fail to even come close.

If your goal is to have a mansion but it seems unbelievable to you, then set your goal to a home that is larger than what you have right now and which will get you excited, but at the same time, feel believable.

THREE MORE TIPS TO VISUALIZATION

If you still struggle to visualize what you want, it's okay. It's actually a good thing. Why? Because struggling to visualize what you want let's you know where your stumbling block is. Since we already know that you can visualize, what you most likely suffer from is the inability to see yourself as deserving of what you want – as worthy.

The **first** tip is something that we already mentioned but is so important that it bears repeating...

You are worthy. You were made in the image of God. You were born worthy. You do deserve to have the life that you want. Remember, it's simply your belief that you aren't that may be holding you back. You deserve to be able to be, do and have anything that you want in life. This is why there are people in the world who are not as smart as you but who are doing better. It's much more about belief than anything else.

Second, instead of visualizing, think of it as imagining. However you use your memory to recall what it is that you want can be used to visualize. Don't get hung up on words like "visualize!"

The **third** thing that you can do is to use a great visualization tool to exercise your visualization muscle.

Here's how to do it...

Look around you right now. Let's say that what is right in front of you is a computer. Try to imprint every detail of your computer right now into your mind so that when you close your eyes, you can still see it. Now close your eyes and try visualize or "imagine" it. Try it now...

Next, open your eyes, see it again and compare it to the vision you had in your head.

Do this a few times until you can see a clearer picture of the object.

The next exercise takes the picture snapshot to the next level of a video recording...

From where you are right now, get up, walk into a room or bedroom, pick up an object like a pillow, touch it, flip it around, and then walk back.

Now, close your eyes and go through the exact same process again, doing your best to recall every minute detail.

Do this multiple times until you can clearly re-play the act in your mind...

This will build up your visualization muscle so that it will be easier for you to create whatever you want.

CREATE A NEW VISION

Now this is where it gets to be more fun. Instead of seeing yourself in environments that you are familiar with, picture, instead, things that you are not. This is why some people choose to create vision boards of their ideal homes, or exotic lands that they have not ever been to. This is where you get to create your reality your way. You get to create whatever you want through the power of your mind.

You are part-creator. You get to choose.

And remember, it's really the feeling that you want to create inside yourself that is going to make it an enjoyable experience. It's a powerful message unto God of what you want that He will not deny.

Ask, and it is given.

CHAPTER 4: ENJOYING THE PROCESS

"Now faith is (the) substantiating of things hoped for, (the) conviction of things not seen." (Heb 11:1, Darby Translation)

What does "enjoying the process" mean?

It means learning to enjoy every aspect, every up and down, and every moment of this process we call life. It means being able to see things from a higher perspective when things are going "bad." And it means enjoying your own growth of character when you face and overcome life's challenges.

It doesn't mean that you have to enjoy the pain of whatever you are going through. What it means is that you can enjoy what the outcome is going to yield for you. When you are tested through a difficult time and you come out of it, you have grown. You character has improved. Who you are as a person is better. You learn from the experience, and you carry the value of what you've been through with you for the rest of your life.

Life has its ups and downs. That is normal. But the odd thing is that most of us trail our feelings behind these external events based upon those ups and downs. In other words, if something "bad" happens, then we feel bad. If something "good" happens, then we choose to feel good. This leads to a life of emotional turmoil and strife. We are tossed around by our sea of emotions, like a ship without a rudder.

But when you learn the value of enjoying the process no matter what, then you can guide your ship to your destination. Then you can steer it to wherever YOU want to go. And then you can become not just the leader of your own being, but the leader of others too...

This chapter is going to explore the highest highs, and the lowest lows, and how you can keep your spirit high no matter what life throws at you.

One of the greatest gifts you will ever receive is the gift of understanding that the "bad stuff" that you experience in life is not bad after all. The "bad stuff," when fully understood, is always beneficial in one way or another.

Hard to believe, right? How could having bad experiences be good? Of what value could it possibly be? When you are in the middle of it all, it feels awful! And it can get to the point where you feel like you just can't go on any longer. Life can get that tough. It can knock you down and rip your heart out while your greatest enemy stands above you and laughs.

Some call this the "dark night of the soul." It's when everything seemingly goes wrong all at once and you're left feeling like a freight train just ran over you. It's also called the "Joseph Calling" or "Joseph Experience."

To many of us who have gone through this, this explanation of what it is like is not an exaggeration! After I tell you my story later in this chapter, you'll understand what I mean...

In chapter 2 when I talked about being down and out, but getting up with a good attitude, that was based on the concept of getting knocked down in life from one thing happening. That chapter was about how when you rise with the right attitude, then you can get back on track – you can fight the good fight – conquer the demons in your life and not just survive but thrive.

Whereas chapter 2 was about what to do when you suffer a blow, this chapter is about when you encounter several blows, one right after the other but then still not only get up with the right attitude, but also, value the experience.

But what if EVERYTHING in your life goes bad *ALL AT ONCE?* How do you handle life then? We aren't talking about just getting knocked to the ground by a good right hook from life – this is more like getting ambushed by 10 people and hanging on for dear life in the end.

The story of Joseph helps us to understand this experience more fully. But just like with anything negative that happens to us, there is a silver lining at the end of this rainbow.

SPIRITUALLY AND FINANCIALLY FREE

In this chapter, we are going to explore why this Joseph Calling is actually a good thing, what you can learn from it, and how to grow from it.

LESSONS FROM AUSCHWITZ

Viktor Frankl was a Jewish psychologist and holocaust survivor. He along with his wife and mother were captured and thrown into different concentration camps. For Viktor, he survived the camps for 4 years where he purposefully studied and documented the human condition of hundreds of other inmates. He did this to understand why some humans survived the most depraved conditions imaginable, while others did not. He must have been thinking that as soon as he got out, he would write about it, which he did.

For him, in his heart, he made up his mind to survive so that he could get back to the love of his life – his wife. His other reason was to help others understand what happened. The love that he had for his wife and the longing he had to see her once again gave him purpose – meaning. His survival instinct kicked in because of her. He endured unimaginable hardship such as countless beatings, having to fight off malnutrition, dealing with tetanus and being forced to dig in frozen earth.

What he found in studying other inmates was that those who gave up thought that they didn't have any reason to live any longer. When they had a reason, they could survive almost anything. When they didn't and they decided to fully give up, they were gone within a day or two.

Your will to live and your WHY are particularly important to not only surviving unfathomable conditions, but also to thrive in a way that helps you to lead a happy and successful life.

Dr. Frankl coined the term "give-up-itis" to those who found no meaning and decided that death was the better option. Typically, they would just lie in bed, allow the guards to beat them, and be gone within a short time.

But when you live a life of meaning and you believe that God will help you endure anything, you summon the strength to go on – to survive – and eventually to thrive too.

One of the less known stories about Viktor Frankl is that one day while he was ready to attain his one meal a day ration, he was handed just a bowl of water with an uncooked fish head in it.

Now, I don't know about you, but for me, I think I would have been a bit disappointed if not disgusted. But Dr. Frankl found beauty in the head of that fish – he found the feeling of appreciation in the most depraved of conditions possible. He was thankful for what was given him. His will power to stay alive knew that the protein in that fish head would allow him to stay alive one more day so that eventually he could return to his beloved wife.

Stripped of all his dignity and worldly possessions, Viktor, reduced to his most basic survival instincts, found a way to survive, and survive he did. But not all stories have a happy ending. After leaving the concentration camp, he found out that both his mom and wife had died in their concentration camps.

The search for meaning for him took on a new meaning. When he got out of the concentration camps, in 1946 he wrote the book "Man's Search for Meaning." Basically, it chronicled his experience as a prisoner in the camps and his psychotherapeutic method which had to do with finding a purpose in life or a reason, your "why" – anything to feel positive about, and then visualizing or imagining that outcome as clearly as possible even if your external conditions were extremely bad.

As sad as that story about Viktor was, the point is that his character was built stronger than ever having survived the concentration camps. He learned much about the human condition and brought understanding to millions through his book about what it was like to survive horrid conditions, and how to do it.

After finding out the outcome for his mother and wife, he wrote a letter to a couple close to him. He wrote, "But I now see things in a larger dimension. I see increasingly that life is so very meaningful, that in suffering and even in failure there must still be meaning. And my only consolation lies in the fact that I can say in all good conscience, that I realized the opportunities that presented themselves to me, I mean to say: that I turned them into reality. This is the case with respect to my short marriage to Tilly. What we have experienced cannot be undone, it has been, but this Having-been is perhaps the most certain form of being."

At one point in the letter he wrote, "There remains perhaps nothing more to do than cry a little and browse a little through the Psalms." He found comfort in the scriptures...

He took opportunities and turned them into reality, even when in a concentration camp. He survived because he kept thinking about his wife, and he kept visualizing himself surviving.

The point of this story is not to make you melancholic or sad, but to impress upon you the vital importance of the human mindset – of our ability to get through anything that life throws at us if we have the right attitude. And that after going through something very trying, your character grows. Who you are as a person improves 10 fold.

Life knocked Dr. Frankl down, but he got back up every single time. He found consolation in God's word. The human spirit, along with God's holy spirit can lift you up after every single knock down. The other point of the story is that Viktor was able to find feelings of appreciation and thankfulness in the most deplorable conditions. When you can conjure up those feelings *REGARDLESS* of what life throws at you, you can then not just overcome anything, but thrive.

Even if you were thrown in prison, if you were to think the right thoughts, pray the right prayers, and clearly visualize the outcome that you wanted, you'd feel freer than a bird. No man can take away your freedom when they cannot break your soul – when they cannot break your spirit. Your spirit is stronger than any external outside condition such as prison walls. When others cannot control how you feel, when you can find happiness in simply being alive no matter what, then no walls can confine you and your inner-being.

YOUR WHY

Why do you do what you do? Why do you get up in the morning? Is it for a loved one? Or loved ones? Is it because you are the head of your family? Or is it because you want to help out your community? Your neighbors? Your state? Your country? Your fellow man? God?

What is your "why?"

Your "why" is what you need to figure out because once you do, you can use that why to motivate and inspire yourself to move forward – to progress – to keep on keeping on.

And then of course, your biggest why could be to be of service to Almighty God, which means being of service to other human beings.

So, think about your why. Who is it? What gets you up in the morning? Why do you do the human thing? Of what purpose is it? When you figure it out, leverage it – use it and find your inspiration there.

Your yearnings and your desires are enough to know that you have a "why" – you just have to figure it out.

LIVE HERE, LIVE NOW

It was Henry David Thoreau who wrote it in his book "Walden" that "the mass of men live lives of quiet desperation." Henry was known for being able to appreciate and find absolute wonder in the mundane – the ordinary – the simple things in his environment – the process of life. It is said that he could find just as much intrigue and beautiful things to see in his own backyard as he could on an adventure to the most remote places on earth...

The point is that he enjoyed the process of life and that he saw how most people were missing the whole point. Most people are not living in the here and now – usually, they do live a life of quiet desperation – either constantly fearful of not making enough money to survive, or of living a life of boredom because they gave up on their own dreams a long time ago.

Enjoying the process is about how to develop the right attitude towards life no matter what is going on.

WHERE CHURCHES FAIL

My belief is that most churches have done their people a complete dis-service by not providing the encouragement, nor the tools to get the most out of life. Many preachers are more concerned about ritual and dogma than they are about truly living and enjoying the process of life that we are all blessed to have.

I'm a bit unconventional that way, but I really think that more churches and preachers need to embrace the self-help aspect of life – to teach their members that it's not only okay to go for your dreams, but that it's essential to your happiness while here on planet earth. God never wanted you to play it small. God never wanted you to lead a mediocre life. Instead, he wants all of us to embrace our co-creative, God-given desire to manifest whatever we want.

Like the potter with the clay, you are the molder of your life. You get to choose to make whatever you want. You get to create your own life. But when religious leaders don't do anything to encourage your creativeness, life can easily start to feel like you're living a life of quiet desperation. Quiet in the sense that you don't even dare tell anyone what you really want for fear that they will judge you. Quiet in the sense that you have given up before you've even started. And desperate in the sense that you know that time is ticking away, leaving you less and less time to create the reality that you really want.

In addition, quiet desperation is having a scarcity mindset and a belief that you cannot change anything. To break free from the shackles of your negative beliefs, you have to be your authentic self by listening to your heart without fear or doubt. God speaks to you through your emotions. You have an emotional guidance system within you that God uses to offer direction and decision-making ability in all aspects of life. The other name for this is your "gut instinct" or intuition.

This is an automatic process. If something feels good to you, it is. If it doesn't, it isn't. It's that simple. Since it never feels good to anyone (even if they deny it) to hurt their fellow human, it's an excellent guidance system. And yet, so many of us let our minds dictate the course of our lives instead of our hearts – our gut instinct.

INTERNAL VS. EXTERNAL LIVING

What is internal versus external living?

External living is valuing, observing, and considering things outside of yourself as more important than what lies within you – internally. External living is being overly concerned about what others think about you, trying to keep up with the Joneses, being overly materialistic, being overly concerned with your looks, worrying about all the things the news media wants you to worry about and more. It's about handing your power over to things that you don't have control of.

Internal living is about understanding that who you are is more important than what you own. It's about connecting with yourself, knowing who you are, being authentic, and trusting in yourself and God. Internal living is about knowing with certainty that everything always turns out well for you, even if externally it may not appear to be true.

Internal living helps you to "enjoy the process" because you understand things such as how failure is part of the process, and how negative events can help you to clarify things like what you really want, or, what not to do next time!

SPIRITUALLY AND FINANCIALLY FREE

When you live your life internally, you are being your true, authentic self and life comes to you much more naturally.

LEADERSHIP

Great leaders never allow outside external things to "rock their boat" to the point where they are an emotional mess because of what happened. Could you imagine what it would have been like for George Washington if he allowed himself to get depressed or sad? He lost more wars than he won, but he never let his emotions get the better of him.

Great leaders are steady and strong, regardless of what is going on. They know that if they allow their emotions to go unchecked, that they would lose focus and even the ability to think. When anyone let's stress get to them, it puts them in a fight or flight state of mind. In this state, blood is diverted from the brain and to the limbs in order to use the energy to run or fight. Thinking literally and physically becomes much more difficult. This is why it's just as important to keep calm in a board room as it is on the battlefield.

Great leaders learn to enjoy the process by having great faith in God that things will always turn out well. They don't have low lows and great highs – they are steady all throughout the process of life. They understand that those that they lead look to them for emotional guidance, and that if they allow themselves to get down, then the energy of the followers will go down too.

But if they are optimistic and positive, then so will everyone else.

Leadership is about being authentic, enjoying the process, not caving in to fear, staying steadfast in their conviction, and trusting in God to bring about the outcome that they want, regardless of circumstances. And of course, it's about enjoying the process no matter how difficult it is because the result is always character building.

CONSTANT PROCESS IMPROVEMENT

If we are to "enjoy the process," one of the additional things to understand is that all of us want constant process improvement. Enjoying the process is the process of getting better at whatever you do, whether that be in your wealth, your health, or in your relationships. But it's also understanding that there will naturally be ups and downs along the way.

At the heart of process improvement is the desire for something better, which we have already established as normal and natural for all human beings – something that none of us should be ashamed of, and something that God wants for us anyway.

Any well-organized company must have as one of the values this concept of process improvement. Without it, the company stagnates and will be surpassed by competing companies.

If all of humanity never embellished the concept of process improvement, we'd all still be riding horses and using candles instead of light bulbs!

SPIRITUALLY AND FINANCIALLY FREE

As you progress through life, your lows and your highs can go higher and higher with process improvement. That is really the only way to fully enjoy the process – it's really enjoying the process of improving yourself and your character in all aspects.

FAITH

At the beginning of this chapter, I quoted Hebrews 11:1 which says, "Now faith is (the) substantiating of things hoped for, (the) conviction of things not seen." (Darby Translation)

Faith is the assured expectation of things hoped for. How is this relevant?

When you have faith, it is much easier to "enjoy the process" because you know that anything that happens will eventually turn out not just okay, but almost always as better in some way. Sometimes, when things go "bad," we have no idea what the lesson is or how it could be for anything good. But God has His plan, and He knows better than us. There is always a good reason – it's just that usually, we can't see it at first.

The next time that something "bad" happens to you, first, tell yourself that it's okay. Remind yourself that there has got to be something beneficial from it and that the benefit will probably not be revealed to you until later. And then have faith that everything is going to turn out alright.

EXAMPLES OF FAITH

Think of the story of David and Goliath in the Bible.

David, just a shepherd body, was the youngest of his brothers but he was fearless. He was known for successfully fighting off lions and bears for the sake of the sheep he was tending to. People of his time thought, if he would do that for sheep, what would he do for his people?

David's brothers were in the army – David would go out to them every day and give them their lunch. He was smaller than all his brothers, but had the heart of a champion...

One day, while running an errand for his father, David found out that Goliath, a Philistine giant, was on the loose taunting and terrorizing the people of Israel. David approached the King and asked why nothing was being done. The King said that there was no one more powerful or ominous than Goliath, and that he could do nothing.

David shocked the King and others when he declared that he would kill Goliath for the people. Many well-meaning ones tried to discourage David from doing anything, explaining that there was no way that he could take on Goliath. He was berated and insulted by those who thought that there was no way he could win. Even his brothers ridiculed him and told him that there was no way he could win. "Who do you think you are!" they yelled at him in both a spirit of anger and jealousy. They told him he was mad and would easily be killed.

But David ignored all of the negativity. He had faith in God that he would be victorious. Undeterred, he went ahead with his plans anyway.

They got him his armor, but he was too small to fit in it and he could barely walk with it on. David thew off the armor and went into battle with Goliath anyway...

The only thing David took with him was his slingshot and 5 smooth stones. Whipping the slingshot around and around, he stood before the giant Goliath and let a stone fly. I think that God took that stone and directed it right through the crack in the head armor of Goliath, landing a fatal blow.

David then ran over to Goliath and triumphantly beheaded him. Focused, determined and driven, he had killed the giant who was much more powerful than him.

David was just a shepherd boy. But he experienced God's helping hand in many ways throughout his life, so when it came to the giant, his faith did not waver.

When you have faith in God, you can overcome any obstacle, no matter how big and scary it may appear to be...

Next, think of the story of Noah and the ark. Up until Noah's day, there was no rain. Instead, there was a canopy of moisture which had a greenhouse effect on planet earth. This allowed men to live until they were 950 years old or so.

But God told Noah that men had become bad – and that every thought of man was evil. God told Noah that he was going to cause it to rain for 40 days and nights and destroy the wickedness that ran rampant on the earth.

Imagine Noah's surprise when he was first told what rain was! Water from the sky? How could that be?

He had to build an ark on dry land, far away from any body of water. Imagine how odd and silly that must have looked to anyone observing him! But he didn't pay any attention to the naysayers. Instead, he listened to God, regardless of how odd it appeared. He had faith in God that what He said was going to come true.

Of course, the rain came, and just before closing the doors to the ark, many of the naysayers became believers, but it was too late for them. Many perished in the flood, and God, seeing the devastation upon the earth, promised that He would never bring that kind of destruction ever again. The rainbow is a sign of that promise.

Sometimes, just as with Noah, you must totally go with your gut instinct on something that may not make any sense to you. But 9 times out of 10, when you do, you will be rewarded with something far better than what you expected.

Think of the times that you may have done something just out of a whim or a "feeling" and it turned out perfectly, or, when you didn't listen to your inner-being and guidance from God and then it didn't turn out well.

We all have those experiences in our lives.

Be like Noah. Listen to God. Listen to your inner-being. Follow your heart. Follow whatever feels good and righteous to you in the moment, and you will never be steered in the wrong direction.

TRAGEDY STRIKES FOR ME

I thought I had the perfect family. My wife and I were married for 25 years, we had three sons, I loved my work, and we were doing well – or so I thought...

But then, things started going bad and we lost our house in a foreclosure. To make matters worse, soon after, my wife informed me that she didn't love me anymore...

She said, "I love you, but I am not *in love* with you..."

And then, I heard the words that every married person dreads to hear when things aren't going well. She said, "I want a divorce."

I was shocked; I couldn't believe it. My "perfect life" was gone in an instant. From there my life went through a series of events that literally almost ended my life twice.

Up until this point, I had the perfect family. I worked every day at a job I loved doing. I had a stable career with a good salary for 25 years, traveling all around the world, speaking at churches, speaking at conferences and doing leadership events.

But suddenly, with just one flip of a divorce switch, I lost it all. I found myself living in an apartment, on my own with no job, no family, and completely broke!

Feeling distraught, confused, upset and disconnected, I asked myself, "How did this happen? Why me? Why now? What did I do to deserve this?!"

I knew that the only thing that could save me was my faith in God and my resolve to get through this most difficult time in my life. Somehow, I had to turn the lemons of my life into lemonade. Life kept on knocking me down to the ground, but I knew that I had to keep on getting back up over and over and over again no matter what came next.

When life crushes you, it can lead to pain, numbing, hatred, bitterness or joy! (James 1:3) You now begin the process of substantiating YOUR Faith. Joy in knowing this will make you a better person, "if you allow it too." Don't expect yourself to be joyful while it's going on – rather, be joyful before and after knowing that it's part of the process. But if you can find joy even while you are going through it, then you have reached a higher spiritual level which will reward you with a happy life no matter what happens.

While you are going through the "dark night of the soul," it is exceedingly difficult to see the light at the end of the tunnel. It is extremely hard NOT to see it as anything but completely "bad" with no value in it whatsoever. But there is great value in it. It builds character. It builds strength. It galvanizes your determination and resolve. And when you include God into the picture, it builds faith.

If there was any one piece of advice I could give anyone going through this is that there is always a silver lining in every cloud. Every negative experience in life has value – a lesson – and is equivalent to fire that is used to purify metal, building character and poise.

I believe I am a much better person today than I was at the beginning of this process. But I had to put away my fear and doubt. I had to embrace the experience and learn from it.

The following is more detail as to what happened to me...

After 30 years, our movement of churches started to fragment because of systemic and autocratic leadership. I knew this wasn't going to be good for me and my family. Being proactive, and living in Atlanta, Georgia, I saw an opportunity to go to London, UK to start a property development company. I was spending 2 weeks a month in both cities. To my joy it went remarkably well. With no capital to start with, I went from "nothing" to $3 million in value over 2 years. I thought I entered the promised land, flowing with milk and honey.

But in 2008, of course, the market crashed. I was leveraged too much; I had to cut my losses and go. Suddenly, I was broke.

Then, I got involved in a multi-level marketing group. It exploded. Then it dried up. Again, suddenly, I was broke...

After that, I started a daycare that had amazing potential. I secured over $100,000 of investment money for it. Then, with the struggling economy, the week that we opened the daycare, we were told that the government was stopping our funding of $16,000 a month. This drastically affected this daycare business. I was broke again! It was at this time that my wife asked for a divorce.

At the same time, sadly my father passed away, and I lost my house all within 7 months. To make matters even worse, I found out that my wife was in a new relationship. I couldn't handle it. It was all too much. Brokenhearted, I moved to California to protect my sons from the potential toxicity of our divorce.

At the time I was thinking, if I couldn't help myself, how could I be a father to my sons? (Today, I wonder if that was the right decision or not. However, that was where I was at the time.)

Through a friend, I got a job working with autistic kids. I did that for 2 years. But a staff member made a mistake with the medicine, I got blamed for it, and then I got fired!

Broke once again...

Then I was the General Manager of two companies that under budgeted for their growth, and they had to let me go. Broke again!!!

Next, I drove for Uber...

Thinking that I could somehow manage to make ends meet by driving people to their destinations, one night, I picked up a lady and started to drive her to her destination. While driving along at 40 mph, a car behind me on my right was about to pass me. But suddenly, that driver swerved into my lane and smashed into the passenger side quarter panel with such force that it turned my car sideways.

Next the car flipped over! When it landed on the roof, all I could hear was a horrendous crash of windows breaking and metal scraping as the car continued to hurl down the street. If it had been during any other time of the day or night, other cars would have hit me...

So, I'm sliding down the road on the roof of my car with my Uber passenger in the back seat! 50 feet of sliding later, when the car finally came to a stop, I looked at my passenger and she was unconscious. I thought for sure she was dead. I unbuckled myself, squeezed through the driver's side door, ran over to her side, opened the door, and managed to get her out.

Thank God she and I were okay. And thank God that there were eyewitnesses to the accident. They reported what they saw to the police and the police report said it wasn't my fault.

Afterward, I sat on the curb holding my head in my hands thinking, what else is going to go wrong? You would think that perhaps I had hit rock bottom by now, but oh no! My dark night of the soul didn't end there!

On another night, while I was working, I accidentally tripped and fell down a storm drain – a 2 foot drop, and landed on my forehead. I laid on the ground for 20 minutes. I could not move or feel my arms and legs. I thought I was paralyzed.

While I was lying face down, I asked God, "Why is all of this happening to me? Why me?"

I literally began to weep from the constant barrage of problems. From 25 years of life security, an amazing family, a beautiful house, and a great neighborhood too, I found myself alone, failing in businesses, rocked from the loss of my dad, the loss of my house, the loss of my wife of 25 years, and the sudden pain from being separated from my boys. I wasn't in my country of origin, had no family, no friends, and I was almost killed twice. I reached a place of utter exasperation: a place of thinking that I was cursed. I had no hope, no life, broken and crushed...

JOSEPH CALLING

Feeling completely exhausted and distraught in life, I then met with a man called Os Hillman who said, "You are going through a Joseph calling." I said, "a what?"

Genesis 37 tells the story of Joseph. He was 17 years old and 2nd youngest of 11 brothers. He told his father, mother, and brothers a dream he had. In this dream, his brothers, mother, and father would bow down to him in the future!! Well, needless to say, that didn't go down too well. This led to a series of events in his life over a span of 13 years. His brothers threw him into a pit and were contemplating whether they should kill him or not!

Instead of killing him, they sold him as a slave to an Egyptian, named Potiphar. Joseph was a handsome young man. While Potiphar was away on business, Potiphar's wife wanted to have sex with him. He refused and while running out of the house, she grabbed his clothing that came off in her hand. She then turned around and accused him of raping her.

He was thrown into jail. But in jail, by being responsible in helping others, he developed a great reputation. Also, he helped interpret dreams. This led to Joseph interpreting Pharaoh's cupbearer's dream who was in jail. Joseph told him that the dream meant he was going to be released and restored back to his position as Pharaoh's cupbearer, which did happen. As the cupbearer was being released from jail, Joseph appealed to him *"Help get me out of here,"* (Gen 40: 14-15) implying he didn't like where he was. Not that anyone likes jail, but it gives you an insight into how Joseph dealt with his own attitude.

He was well liked and helpful to people, no matter where he was. But the cupbearer forgot about him for 2 years until Pharaoh had a dream that none of his wise men could explain. Finally, the cupbearer remembered Joseph. Pharaoh had him brought out of prison, to interpret the dream, which he did. This led to Joseph becoming the number 2 guy in all of Egypt. Part of the interpretation of his dream was that there would be a famine in the land. Joseph prepared to store grain for Egypt. When the famine hit the land, all nations came to Egypt begging for help.

Part of all the nations who came begging for help were Joseph's father, mother and brothers who didn't recognize him, but bow downed to him, appealing to him for food, shelter and help, thus fulfilling his initial dream. Joseph was not vindictive towards his brothers, in fact, he was humbled by seeing them, so much so that he had to excuse himself from their presence so he could weep with joy!

Os shared with me how throughout the Bible, God allowed certain men to go through hardships because he had a greater plan for them. This was called the "Joseph Calling."

Genesis 49:22-24 says, *"Joseph is a fruitful vine, a fruitful vine near a spring, whose branches climb over a wall. With bitterness, archers attack, they shoot at him with hostility. But his bow remained steady, his strong arms stayed, limber, because of the hand of the mighty one of Jacob, because of the shepherd, the rock of Israel."*

This is a description of how Joseph's life looked – like a snapshot of the events in his life. It describes him as a fruitful vine that rises above a wall. It shows that he rose above his problems; he was not crushed by them. He didn't try to go through a wall but instead, found ways to glide over it. His fruit was trusting God and not letting fear or bad circumstances affect him poorly. His steadiness and confidence, while archers were trying to kill him, came from his belief in God.

Joseph dealt with a lot of challenges in his life, but he handled everything with grace and peace. He saw it as training from God. He knew it was about God and character. He had a different mindset than others. He understood the process and enjoyed it.

Men like Joseph, David, Jeremiah, Elijah, Daniel and many more went through really tough times that ended up glorifying God.

Os shared with me about his own life. He owned a printing company that went very well. He had a terrific lifestyle, but then, it came crashing down. He lost a half million, his marriage, his house and was estranged from his daughter. He found himself in a place, like me. From there, Os spent 7 years in hardship. Then God opened the doors. He built a business of helping businessmen all around the world. He began writing a devotional every morning about his struggles. He emailed it to a few businessmen he knew. That email list grew to 250,000! God restored all his losses, except his marriage, however. But he found a woman that became the love of his life. I have to say this gave me hope and courage to move on. And it taught me how much we need each other.

With my new understanding, he gave me a new attitude – that God had never left me although, at times, I felt he did. Now, God is calling me to serve him in a different way. Firstly, to change my thinking, understanding there is a bigger purpose going on. He is leading me to get in touch with my gifts and passion. Then, how to use them to serve others with my life and to begin to understand "Enjoying the Process."

Enjoying the process is all about no matter what life throws at you, your attitude, mindset and character doesn't change. You start to see a bigger picture. You start to say, "I don't wish for life to get easier; I wish for Me to get better." To what extreme these challenges go varies from person to person, but you start to believe this is a process not a curse! It starts to feel like God is calling you by setting the sails of your boat, which then catches the winds to move you, thereby substantiating your faith. This is "Enjoying the Process."

MORE CHARACTER BUILDING STORIES

Christopher Helps Me Grow

Today, my oldest son Christopher stands at 6' 8". He was always a tall child. Coaches loved him and begged him to play basketball. One coach at high school followed him around the school begging him to play.

I remember when I first took him to play basketball when he was seven years old. He was much taller than all the rest of the kids. He would run up and down the basketball court just fine, but he wasn't focused. He would look up at the ceiling and wave at me, but not really participate in the game. So, I said to him that if he scored 5 baskets that I would get him an ice cream after the game. He said, "If you make it two, then I will score the baskets." I said all right...

In an instant, he transformed from a non-focused kid to a scoring demon. He started yelling and screaming for the basketball and started scoring baskets. Every basket he scored he'd look over at me and say one, two, three, etc... I started to fantasize, "I have an NBA star on my hands! I just have to figure out how to keep him focused and motivated."

Then, we watched a friend of mine coaching a team. He called a timeout and was enthusiastically yelling at and motivating the team. Christopher leaned over to me and said, "Dad, they are always shouting at each other."

I said "Yes! Yes! That gets everyone fired up! Isn't that great?"

He said "No, I don't like it. I hate sports!"

At that moment, my heart sank and all my dreams of my son becoming an NBA star were flushed down the toilet. I begged God, please don't curse me with a giant who hates sport! Since I was always into sports such as boxing and soccer, of course, naturally, I wanted that for my son. I loved all aspects of sports, including the camaraderie that you have in the locker room and I wanted that for my son too.

So, when Christopher said that he didn't like sports, I thought, how could this be? No God, not me, please. But it was to be... My oldest and tallest son was a hater of sports...

I really struggled with this. What did I do wrong that caused him to not have an appreciation for sports? Should I have started him sooner? Or should I have not pushed him into it at all and let him decide if he wanted to do it or not? Should I have just been the example and not ever pressed it? Should I impose my beliefs on him?

After a while of thinking about it, I started to realize that Christopher was not me. His experience in life was different than mine, by far. He lived in a different time, a different set of circumstances, a different social environment, different schools, friends, etc.... There were too many outside influences that I had no control over. If I was to be God-like in how I treated him, I had to be unconditionally loving. I had to realize that it is never a good idea to live vicariously through your offspring, but a much better idea to accept and embrace who they truly are and what they love – not what I love.

I started to think that as a father I needed to focus on what he wants, not what I want. He was super creative. I started to recognize this when he dressed up for Halloween at school. Most children would nag their parents to buy them a Halloween outfit. But Christopher loved the idea of creating his own outfit.

One Halloween in the morning before school, he painted his face and legs black then stepped into a black bin liner.

I said, "What is that?"

He said, "I am a black current."

I started to laugh because it was clever, creative and funny. Then I started to worry, "What will the other kids say about him? Aren't they going to tease him to no end?" But I knew I had to let that thought go because if kids did tease him, who am I to keep him from a valuable experience of character building?

Off he went to school dressed as a black current. I watched him walk up the street to school and when I finally came to a good feeling place about it, I thought to myself, "What a creative young chap he is. He views life so different than me."

But of course, that wasn't the only time I'd be challenged to be an unconditionally loving father...

One day, he arrived home carrying a stop sign.

I opened the door and said, "Where are you going with that?"

He said, "I thought it would look great in my bedroom!"

I sarcastically asked, "Do you have cars driving through your bedroom?"

He said, "Dad, it makes my bedroom unique."

I said, "It does that for sure. Where did you get it?"

He said, "I found it in the street."

I said, "You know that's illegal – to take government property..."

He said, "No one will know..."

I said, "I know! Go and put it back!"

So, he did...

I was really having a hard time being patient with Christopher. He saw life from a totally different viewpoint than me... Was life a lesson for him, or was he a lesson for me?

Another day he came home with a huge boulder...

I said, "Where are you going with *that*?"

"The bedroom," he said.

I said, "What is it about your bedroom you don't like?"

"I want more character in it," he said.

I thought that the only one getting more character here is me, not his bedroom!

Another story is when I had my daycare, I needed the walls to be painted. Christopher offered to paint one of them, so I let him.

When he showed it to me, I was almost in a state of shock. He had painted Gothic characters on the wall, and part of it looked like a bomb had gone off.

I said, "Why couldn't you paint something like Bugs Bunny or Donald Duck instead of this?"

But he explained to me that "this is the good stuff Dad!"

Then mothers came out of the daycare and looked in horror at his painting and I said, "Does that look like she thinks this is the 'good stuff'?!"

As time went on, and after struggling with accepting Christopher for who he was, I realized that we could connect with each other through music...

So, I taught Christopher the guitar. I taught him some of the basic chords. But then he decided he didn't like the basic chords, so he created his own chords. To me, that was extraordinary and remarkable. Then, he fell in love with writing songs. He has probably written 200 songs or more. I remember one song called "the blind preacher man." That certainly caught my attention since I was a preacher for 25 years.

I went to visit a friend who wanted to record me singing some songs, so I brought Christopher. After I recorded my songs I said to Christopher, "Do you want to record?"

He said "Yes," and he sang "the blind preacher man."

Unaware to Christopher and me, there was a Georgia Tech, music student there who recorded Christopher's song. That student brought the song to lecture the next day. They studied how Christopher wrote music. It was profound. About then, I started to realize just how creative Christopher was, and that perhaps there was a creative genius in him that I had been overlooking.

Another story is that one time I had the keyboard player of "The Rolling Stones" in my Uber car. I told him about Christopher and he asked if he had saved any songs. I said no. He said that is crazy! And he then asked, "Why doesn't he save any of his songs?" I had to agree! Why didn't he save any of his songs? Why wasn't he thinking in terms of being able to sell his music or do something more with it?

It baffled me. But again, I realized, that's Christopher's choice – not mine. Maybe he was here to help me to learn to live more in the moment and not try to make money from every creative ability.

Another story is that Chris moved out of the house when I was in LA – he invited me to come for a visit. He lived in a basement of a building – of a factory.

I went down to see him, and the first thing about it was that from the street, you could only see the top-half of the door. You literally had to jump down to get to the level where the entrance was.

It was very dark in there. His hippy friends were all around. The place was segmented by curtains with no walls. I thought, "This is a death trap."

We went to his room which was very small and tidy, to my surprise. He said, "Dad, it's tidy, because one night at 2 am in the morning I was in a deep sleep and I woke up and heard your voice say to me, 'Your room is a reflection of who you are as a person.' And Dad, it was a mess. So, I jumped out of bed and immediately cleaned my room up to what it is today!"

I was encouraged with that. Christopher has a pure heart; he is a gentle giant. He really touches my heart. I saw this too when we worked with autistic kids together. He was amazing with them.

I started to figure out that it's not the son who has to change, but the dad. Christopher wasn't the issue – it was me. Our children want to grow, but usually, they want to grow when they are ready.

I should have trusted the process more with Christopher. When he realized that he could get a rise out of me, sometimes, he would do it on purpose and then have a laugh about it with his friends. The truth was, I had to learn to suck it up – learn to not let him get the best of me for any reason. At some point, I made up my mind not to react to anything ever again, but it's still a struggle!

When I came across strong against Christopher, I wasn't being gracious. I wasn't following the example of Jesus. I wasn't trusting that God would speak to Christopher and let him know that I was a good dad just doing the best I could.

The hardest thing for a dad is to suck it up! We are so used to setting rules and limits for the growth and protection of our children, that we sometimes lose sight of allowing our children to embrace the creative side of themselves.

I have to constantly think that it is me that has to change. Matt 7:12 says to *"do to others what you would have them to do you."* That is the golden rule. So, we must treat our sons and daughters as you would want to be treated. When you get out of the way, they will either learn on their own from their mistakes, or they will follow your loving example from a place of not forcing them in one direction or another.

You can never give up hope as a parent. Parents have got to be secure in the thought that there is no one else more influential than them in their children's life – either good or bad.

I hear from other parents that their children are quite different than they are too – they have the same struggles – it's almost like the new ones coming in demand and expect a certain amount of freedom that we never really had before – and that perhaps it is very beneficial to look at old things like the standard chords of a guitar and create new ones. Or, perhaps the yelling and screaming to motivate someone to do something is not the best route to go...

There is a saying from a basketball coach that goes, "It's better to light a fire within a players heart, rather than light one under his feet."

Maybe Christopher was right after all...

But what I learned from Christopher was that life can be experienced and seen through many different ways and angles – no better or worse than my view. I respected Christopher's view of life, and part of me could understand why he did what he did, and how being creative beings, we should be allowed to create whatever experience we want.

His unconventional way of looking at life got me to love and accept him for who he was, and to admire him for not following the strict, regimented, structured, boring ways of the world – the world that I had grown up in...

Christopher helped me be a better parent. I had to look at life the way he saw it – not the way I saw it...

Shane Builds Character

When Shane was seven years old, he wanted to play football. He wanted to play quarterback. On the first day, they divided the kids up into where they felt by size they would fit best. Shane was selected to be part of the defensive team. After his first practice he said, "I don't like being in the defensive team; I want to be quarterback."

I said OK let's go over and talk to the coach then. The coach was a guy called Dave Savula, a great guy. I turned to Shane and said, "Shane, tell Coach Savula what you told me..."

Without hesitation, Shane said, "I want to be quarterback."

Coach Savula said to him, "We have six quarterbacks as it is."

Shane said, "Then why don't you make it seven?"

Coach Savula started to laugh at Shane's answer. But then said, "Because of your attitude, I will make it seven."

By the end of the season Shane was the starting quarterback. He had a great desire to learn so I got coaching lessons from a friend of mine who was the starting quarterback of Duke – a guy named Kevin Thompson. He was very helpful to Shane and really spent a lot of time on Shane's footwork.

Then I took Shane to football camps and they singled out Shane and how great his technique and foot work was.

In high school, in his freshman, sophomore and junior year, he was the starting quarterback. He was really looking forward to being the starting quarterback in his senior year. But the coach made a change to another kid because he wanted to play a running game and not a throwing game because a strong arm wasn't necessary.

Shane was known as the gunslinger because he had such a great arm. It was a great disappointment to him and to me as a dad. I hurt for him.

I wanted to see how Shane would react during the season. Would he be disappointed and feel sorry for himself? Or would he hold up his head high and not allow external conditions get him down?

I'm glad to say that he showed great character. He was genuinely nice to the new quarterback, and very happy for him. He showed great personality in the locker room too.

Sadly, one of his teammates was killed through an automobile accident. The coach asked if any of the kids would like to share at the funeral. Shane put his hand up and said that he would like to share...

He did an amazing job speaking in front of about 600 students and parents sharing how great and encouraging this young man was and told some very funny stories about the practices and how his teammate was awesome – to the point that the family afterwards hugged Shane and said how grateful they were to share those things about their son. I was so proud of Shane – what a fine young man he was, taking it upon himself to share that so openly.

This gave me an insight into what kind of character Shane had. He went on to college, did his undergraduate degree but then went on to do his masters and CPA in the same year and passed with flying colors. A lawyer and friend of mine said that to do your masters and CPA in the same year is as hard as trying to pass the bar. He was headhunted by Ernst and Young (one of the top four auditing companies in the world) and held up as "this is the kind of kid we're looking for in our company." He was lifted up as a leader and was given a lot of responsibility.

The point is that disappointments and tough circumstances are not bad. They are the building blocks to a great character if you have the right attitude, vision and purpose for your life. Shane showed me this in a powerful way through his high school years.

SPIRITUALLY AND FINANCIALLY FREE

My Lessons from "Enjoying the Process"

Holy Spirit

The Holy Spirit's goal in pointing us to Jesus is to replace the destruction of deception in our lives with the wholeness of truth. By leading us into an experience of truth, the Holy Spirit works to counteract the experiences in our lives that root us in the deception of the flesh. The result is that the fruitless deeds of darkness are replaced with "the fruits of the light... Goodness, righteousness and truth." (Eph 5:9) There are, I believe, several interrelated ways by which the spirit produces this wholeness in our lives.

Experiencing God

Firstly, the more we experience the truth of who God is and the truth of who we are in Christ, the more our experienced self-identity becomes restored to the beautiful God dependent relationship for which we were originally created. Our need for love and worth is increasingly met as we grow in our dependency on the one who alone can meet it. We become human beings instead of human doings, for our worth is established in who we are, rather than in what we do. As we experience the inherent love that God has towards us and the worth God gives to us, we increasingly come to reflect this love and the worth in our own identities. As we experience the truth, Wholeness replaces destruction in our lives. This is when you begin to "Enjoy the Process."

Stop Performing

Secondly, once we see the truth of who God is and the truth of who we are in Christ, we can then overcome the unhealthy separation between our inner selves and our external selves that the performance mentally created in our lives.

The more we experience the truth that our love and worth are a settled issue, not dependent upon our performance, the less we need to perform. In other words, we are born worthy as children of God, complete and whole in His image. As we get our innermost needs met by God, we are free from trying to get life from idols. Hence, we begin to live as we were created to live: as emotionally healthy young children live before society teaches them to do otherwise. And then what happens is that we begin to live on the outside what is true on the inside.

Healing

Thirdly, the closer our inner and outer realities come into agreement, the more the issues that needed healing are exposed and can be openly addressed. As we experience the truth of who God is and the truth of who we are in Christ, our need to conceal our wounds and struggles disappear. Since our value is established by grace, we no longer need to try to win it by our good works. Therefore, we can risk vulnerability, both before God and before others within the body of Christ. This too is wholeness confronting and overcoming destruction.

THE CHARACTER BUILDING PROCESS

One of the last things that I wanted to mention about the character-building process is that when you can humble yourself to the criticisms of others, you build more character. You will always have haters, no matter what you try to do or accomplish in life – especially if you get into the public eye.

But one of the things that I have learned is that if you can be objective to the criticisms of others, you can grow from it – you can learn.

Sometimes, your critics are your best guides because those who love us and who are close to us will not want to hurt us with the truth. But if you can take the criticism, acknowledge it, and even admit at times that they are right, you will be able to diffuse the haters to some degree, gain the respect of some, and then truly grow.

There is never any shame in admitting when you are wrong – to the contrary, it is the sign of a person with strong character, high morals, and high integrity.

When you understand that all of us are constantly growing, then there is no shame in admitting when you might be wrong.

Chapter 5: Why Believe the Bible?

Shane was 5 years old. He was cute and rambunctious. We had just moved into a house in Northern Virginia – a place called Great Falls. It was the first house we ever lived in that had a swimming pool.

My 3 sons were very fired up about having a swimming pool. There was great excitement about our first day allowing them to get into the pool. Christopher was eight years old; Shane was five and Joshua was two. But none of them could swim. Christopher ran around the outside of the pool, eager to get in.

I was carrying Joshua and putting some floaties on his arms. Then, out of nowhere, Shane decided to indulge in his rambunctiousness...

While I was paying attention to Joshua, I heard a splash at the deep end of the pool. I looked around and couldn't see Shane. Suddenly I realized, it was Shane who jumped into the pool. He couldn't swim and he chose to jump in the deep end!

I nearly dropped Joshua on his head! I quickly put Joshua down, ran and dove into the pool. Shane was already at the bottom of the pool. I grabbed him and lifted him out of the water. As I looked at his face, he wiped the water from his eyes and then put on a big smile. I was exasperated and said, "What are you doing?! You can't swim. You jumped in the deep end!"

He said, "I knew you would come!"

I had no words to say...

Then Christopher said "Dad, this is going to be great, we can swim here every day!"

I said "No, we are shutting the pool down. I am putting the canopy over this pool so that no one can use it!"

Christopher said "Dad!"

I was afraid in my heart that Shane would wake up at two in the morning and jump in the pool and expect me to come and save him. There was no way I was allowing this pool to be used.

Shane had said, I trust you dad! But that was trust I couldn't live with!

Shane frightened the life out of me.

But Shane had *total trust and faith in me.* Imagine if we had that kind of faith in God – to be able to jump into the deep end of life and to know that He would save us if we failed...

Having no fear like Shane is in a way courageous. When we trust the Bible even with its inconsistencies, God will come to you and make things clearer. Your faith is built upon the experiential moments of your life, guided by the Bible and the Holy Spirit.

But why can you trust in the Bible? What's your view on the Bible? Is it a holy book? What is the purpose of reading it? Is it inspired by God? Most strict evangelical groups would say, it's divinely inspired. You must believe in everything the Bible says. "There are no errors in the Bible."

Yet, I have found errors, inconsistencies, and things that are hard to understand. I've found images of God that is not like Jesus. You may say, "Chris, you are a believer. Won't questioning the Bible and showing errors destroy people's faith?"

I questioned a lot of things in life but there was a long period that I accepted everything while working for the church and its questionable leadership. I believe it significantly hurt my faith, my marriage and family. I had faith in a church structure, in a community, and in a mission, but daily, I didn't have personal faith in Jesus. I believed the Bible but never questioned some of the glaring concerns about it.

When you aren't even allowed to question something, how is that okay? How is that not like a cult where the leaders force you to believe a certain way and to "take their word for it?"

My feeling is that the truth should be strong enough to handle all questioning, and that it is not a sign of lack of faith to question, rather, it is a sign of strength. How?

If you have questions about your faith in your heart that are not answered, your faith is not strong. But when you question matters and then answer your own questions that supports your faith, then your faith is stronger than ever.

I never believed in blindly following anyone or anything. We are all in the process of expansion of understanding and seeing things from a different angle. When men thought that the earth was flat, you could be hung if you stated anything otherwise. And yet, the entire time, the earth wasn't flat.

How can you progress in life if you don't answer obvious questions that arise? And why is it that diametrically opposed thoughts can't co-exist? In other words, why can't the Bible be inspired of God, but have a few errors in it because it was translated by imperfect humans?

Regardless of how I felt about the Bible, I used it for inspiring insights, to gain knowledge to teach the congregation, and to support my beliefs. But I also used it to prove other beliefs wrong. It was something like a tech book. But it was all head knowledge – not enough heart and experiential knowledge.

I was religious, but questioning the Bible led me to believe in Jesus, then the Bible. I believe this is a better approach because Jesus believed in the inspiration of the Bible. In turn, believing in Jesus first helped me see how God mentors people through imperfection – mentoring us to fix our eyes on Jesus, the author and perfecter of our faith. I had the base belief in the Bible *because* of Jesus, not the other way around.

Now, I'd like to show you why I think the Bible is inspired in spite of errors and inconsistencies. But then, I'm going to show you the other side of the coin and show you where there are glaring inconsistencies that unbelievers can easily point to. How would you answer their questions?

But first, let's cover why I think the Bible is inspired.

ARGUMENTS FOR BIBLICAL INSPIRATION

We have compelling historical reasons to accept that the early disciples were not lying and were not passing on a legend. We thus have compelling historical reasons to accept that the Gospels are basically reliable and to therefore accept that Jesus is Lord...

Jesus clearly believed the old testament was the inspired word of God and he pre-authorized the New Testament as inspired by God. The Holy Spirit will lead them into all truth.

If we confess Jesus as Lord, we are not free to correct his theology, especially on such a foundational matter as the inspiration of Scriptures.

Conclusion: all who confessed Jesus to be Lord must consider the Old and the New Testament to be the inspired word of God.

Paul says at 2 Timothy 3:16-17, *"All Scripture is God breathed and is useful for teaching rebuking correcting and training in righteousness so that the man of God might be thoroughly equipped for every good work."*

The term "God breathed" is unique in that it is saying God breathed it out. These words are from God, referring to the Bible as divinely inspired by God. I am going to be looking at the questionable aspect of the Bible. Therefore, it begs the question, how is this "God breathed" or divinely inspired?

If you are an evangelical Christian, you tend to believe the Bible is a perfect book, with no errors, no mistakes, free of controversy and historically accurate. The litmus test for Evangelical Christians is, "If you don't believe this, then you don't believe in the Bible." They believe that the Bible cannot possibly have errors. The argument or assumption goes that if God breathed it, and God is perfect, then his book, the Bible, must be perfect!

On one hand, this make sense and is reasonable. This is an assumption though, made by man. Yet, many times God does exactly the opposite of what man thinks. This is a misguided argument. It's a dangerous point of view and it set people up to fall. When a professor, friend, or a scholarly person is critical of the Bible because it shows inconsistencies, it destroys people's faith. More young people lose their faith because of this more than anything else. They don't know how to deal with the mistakes and inconsistencies in the Bible.

When I went through my hardships and saw inconsistencies with the Bible, leadership and Church culture, it almost destroyed my faith. I was angry with God, because other people in leadership were affecting my life by quoting Bible verse that didn't feel like the spirit of Jesus. They only taught methods and programs.

It upset me so much that I went to a park, to a specific low hanging, "Weeping Willow Tree" that I used to pray under. I screamed at God; I beat the ground. I yelled at God, shouting, "Where are you? Why are things so confusing? So many points of view. Is the Bible real or not? How can so many people make a strong argument on both sides of truth?"

This was a problem because I didn't understand the argument that I am addressing in this chapter which is that "God works through imperfection." There are mistakes and inconsistencies in the Bible that I am going to show you. But also, I will show you that this is how God moves towards building a relationship with us. It's a beautiful story of God's love for us and how He wants to have a deep abiding relationship with us.

Here are samples of some of the problems I am talking about. I am going to show that these imperfections will strengthen your faith, not hurt it so you are better equipped to deal with inconsistencies in your own faith.

ARGUMENTS FOR BIBLICAL ERRORS

Cosmology or science says that the Bible is wrong – it's not a science book. Here's the evidence:

The sky is a "dome" that is *"hard as molten mirror"* (Job 37:18), for it separates *"the waters that were under the dome from the waters that were above the dome"* (Gen 1:7).

The dome rests on Pillars, as does the earth as it sits upon the *"waters"* that encircle it. (Ps 104:2-3, 5-6, cf. Job 9:6, 26:11, Ps 75:3).

Yahweh opens *"windows"* in the solid dome when Yahweh wants it to rain, allowing the waters *"above the dome"* to fall to the ground (Gen 7:11;8:2; Isa 24:8; Mal 3:10).

The Sun, Moon and Stars are all *"lights in the dome"* that were placed there to function as *"sign and for seasons and for days and years"* (Gen 1:14).

In dealing with ancient cosmology, they preached as they saw things. It was their perception. They didn't have the science we have today. The sky was a dome – a blue dome that holds up the water. Earth sits on big pillars. A good question then is, what do the pillars stand on? This was the Scientology's eastern view. We know that not to be true. When you look up into the sky, you are looking into a vast space, out into a galaxy that's part of a universe. We know this because of our science and advancement today. The ancient world had no idea. Their science was wrong. These show inaccuracies in the Bible.

But how were the inspired men of the Bible going to explain it from their limited knowledge of what reality was? Could it be that even though they got it wrong, that it was simply their own imperfect filtering of the information from God that transpired, rather than God being wrong?

But wait. There is more...

The Bible talks about mythological sea monsters such as Leviathan, Behemoth, and Rahab:

Leviathan has many heads (Ps 74:14).

Blows smoke out of its nose(s) and fire out of its mouth(s) (Job 41:18-21).

Even "the gods are overwhelmed at the sight of him" (Job 41;9).

This monster can eat iron like straw and crush bronze like it was decayed timber (41:26-27).

Only God can subdue this creature, and even he needs a sword (Isa 27:1; Job 40:19).

We understand now that these were myths. However, the Bible describes them as creatures. Leviathan was a multi-headed sea monster that lived in the seas. It came out of the sea to cause problems. It was responsible for natural disasters, disturbing oceans, winds, earthquakes, and it was behind the chaos in the ancient known world. Behemoth was a sort of huge, contoured rhinoceros along with Rahab, another ancient creature. They were frightening creatures that where responsible for the trouble on the earth. But there weren't such creatures; it was an effort to describe Satan and his cosmic forces of evil. Did the men who wrote the Bible expect us to understand that it was all symbolism and not to be taken literally? If not, then again, the Bible is inaccurate.

Here are other contradictions in the Bible:

At 2 Sam 24:1 the Lord incites David to sin by counting his army.

But at 1 Chron 21:1 Satan incites David to sin by counting his army.

Who incites David? Was it God, or Satan?

When tempted, no one should say, "God is tempting me." For God cannot be tempted by evil, nor does he tempt anyone (James 1:13).

James says, God can't tempt anyone to do evil. I believe in the Chronicle version; the writer looked back and saw there was something evil influencing David. God said *"Don't put your trust in your sword or horse but in me."* David was not trusting God. Why? Maybe out of fear, or anxiety. It's interesting that every time in the Old Testament that an Israelite used the sword, they were not trusting God:

Ex 34:7/ Num 14:18 says God *"visits the iniquity upon the parents of the children and the children's children, to the third and fourth generation."*

But Ezk 18:20 says: *"A child shall not suffer for the iniquity of a parent, nor the parent suffer for the iniquity of a child; the righteousness of the righteous shall be his own, and the wickedness of the wicked shall be his own."*

In other words, Moses says one thing, a few hundred years later Ezekiel says the complete opposite. What's the answer? Could it be that God was becoming more and more loving as time passed? Or is this a direct contradiction? I don't know! It is what it is!

And then, there are human mistakes in the Bible (Paul, Mark and Matthew: clear mistakes):

1 Cor 1:14-16: *"I thank God I baptized none of you except Crispus and Gaius, so no one can say you were baptized in my name. (I did baptize the household of Stephanas, beyond that, I do not know whether I baptized anyone else.)"* The apostle Paul has a loss of memory. He forgot who he baptized. How could he forget? What else could he forget?

Mark 1;2: *"As it was written in Isiah the prophet, 'Behold' I am sending you my messenger before your face, who shall prepare your way."* The correct reference is to Malachi 3;1.

Mark 2;26: *"Have ye never read what David did... how he went into the household of God in the days of Abiathar the high priest, and did eat the shewbread, which is not lawful to eat but for the priest?"* The correct reference is to Ahimelech, Abiathar's father (1 Sam 21: 1-6).

Matt 27;9-10: *"Then what was spoken by Jeremiah the prophet was fulfilled: 'They took the thirty pieces of silver, the price set on him by the people of Israel, and they used them to buy the potter's field, as the Lord commanded me.'"* The actual reference is to (Zechariah 11;13).

Unchrist-like images of God:

Deuteronomy 20: 16-17 says *"However, in the cities of the nations the Lord your God is giving you as an inheritance, do not leave alive anything that breathes. Completely destroy them—the Hittites, Amorites, Canaanites, Perizzites, Hivites and Jebusites—as the Lord your God has commanded you."* Kill everything that breathes? That means men, women, and children! How does this image of God look compared to God at the cross who sacrificed his Son for humanity? Were people that evil that God had to destroy everyone? Or did God get progressively more lenient with his people? Again, I don't know.

If we assume a perfect God would reveal himself in a perfect book, then these facts are going to trouble you because there's a lot of human error involved in these details. The all-important question is, *why should we assume we know what a perfect God looks like and what his perfect book should read like?*

God always does the opposite of what man thinks. We don't know anything when it comes to God. We need to stop assuming. When God responded to Job, he asked Job, were you there when I hung the Moon, Sun, Stars and separated the Oceans? The answer was no. Job was questioning God. He was angry at God because he didn't understand. God was telling Job you have no idea what is involved in running the universe with evil involved and allowing man to have free will.

Man has a lust for power, greed, and control. We should not assume God is the same. It is dangerous for us to assume we know how God would act. For instance, the Jewish nation thought that the Messiah was going to be born into royalty and grow up with a privileged life, destroy the Roman Empire and elevate the Jewish nation.

The Messiah was also supposed to consolidate the religious world and condemn the sinners.

God did the complete opposite. Jesus was born into poverty, lived a pauper's life, condemned the religious order, befriended sinners and let the Romans crucify him. This isn't what the Jews expected; it isn't what man would do. This looks offensively weak, but this is what God will do. The fullest revelation of God and his power is the Cross! *Let God teach us.*

The Jews were wrong on every account. The Cross is the epicenter of God teaching us about a perfect God. The full revelation of God is seen at the Cross. All scripture, both the Old and New Testament, point towards the Cross as the full revelation of a perfect God.

3 THINGS THE CROSS TEACHES US

1) God is Comfortable Looking Weak

If you asked a group of people "What would it look like for God to show his omnipotent-self?" the vast majority would say, "It would be impressive, shock, awe and have a wow factor about it, like, lifting Africa out of the earth and spinning it around like pizza dough."

"For the message of the cross is foolishness to those who are perishing, but to us who are being saved, it is the power of God.... But we preach Christ crucified, a stumbling block to Jews and foolishness to Gentiles, but to those whom God has called, both Jews and Greeks,

Christ the power of God and the wisdom of God" (1 Cor 1:18, 23-24).

If you too thought that God would do something miraculous to prove his existence, you would be wrong. "The Cross" is the power of God! Humans have lust for power, not God. All Christians throughout time have struggled to accept this because love looks weak. Surrender looks weak. Humility looks weak. It's not what the world values or respects. Winning and conquering is everything. This is what looks powerful in the world. It is short term value and short term gain. Churches want to see churches winning and conquering the world.

"Evangelizing the world in our generation" is a quote that I have heard thrown around a lot. The Cross looks weak and stupid to the world. If God looks foolish and weak at the Cross, why wouldn't we assume, that the book he created seems foolish and weak? The Cross should tell us 'God breathed' through imperfect people and they aren't an obstacle to God getting his message out. If God breathed through Jesus dying on the Cross, which embody all the sin and imperfection in the world, then this is found in Jesus at the Cross.

What we should learn is this: the power of an omnipotent God comes to the world and reveals his power as self-sacrificial love that looks foolish and weak. If this is true, then we should assume he is comfortable revealing himself this way!

2) God is Relationship Driven

Here is why things get mixed up. Humans assume that everything comes unilaterally from God. If we learn anything, 'Gods breathing' isn't unilateral; it is relational. God breathes through imperfect people who share with other imperfect people. This isn't unilateral; it is relational. That's why God's word gets mixed up with fallen and sinful stuff. God's moving towards people by becoming a human then allowing them to crucify him – that is God moving in a relational dynamic. Allowing people to act towards him, beating and killing Jesus, God humbly accepts them. It's a beautiful demonstration of God's love for us. He allows the sinful nature of the world to act towards him, so that he can build a relationship with us; this is relational.

The Cross mirrors the ugliness of the world. If God's fullest revelation comes through the one who bears all sin in the world, shouldn't we read the Bible knowing God's breathing is going to be relational? We need to see the Cross as center and read the Bible knowing that it's God acting towards us allowing people, which includes the Biblical authors, to act towards him and allow them to condition through God's breathing how he is viewed or perceived. This is the relational work of God. God will not coerce us into believing him. Shouldn't we read the Bible like it's BEAUTIFUL, God acting toward us, UGLY and WEAK when we act towards him? Everyone acknowledges the individual qualities of the character's writing the Bible. God allows them to condition his message through their perception, culture and character. They were independent from each other.

We can see that God works with individuals, allowing them to communicate through their imperfect way. God is perfect, his language is perfect, but he is comfortable letting broken people communicate his message. It's not unilateral, like one language, being poured into vessels. There are a lot of personalities writing, working with God, co-working with God, and allowing them to condition how the Bible was written. Mark's Greek is pretty raw. Paul's is much better. God is perfect but allowed Mark to educate the world about him.

This clearly communicates that God did not feel the need to course correct Mark's Greek. So, Mark communicated imperfect Greek, God breathed that, but God is perfect. Paul's memory loss in (1 Corinthians 1:14-15) is not perfect but God allowed Paul's communication to educate the world. God is not a coercive God; he did not feel the need to course correct Paul's memory before he wrote the book. God breathed through Paul's imperfect memory. God does not lobotomize people; he works with them as they are. God allows his message to be seen as imperfect as people choose to read or listen. If we use the Cross as a paradigm, we can see that God is comfortable working with imperfection. The world may not be, but God is.

We should not assume we know God. God enters into solidarity with us through the Cross – he stooped down to our level to connect with us through relationship. If

God's perfect message can be communicated through the imperfect Jesus dying on the cross, Jesus carrying all the ugliness of the world, why would He have a problem with the inconsistencies with Mark, Matthew and Paul's memory? All of this contributes to the inspiration of the Bible – that God would work with all of us, stoop down to our level and love us just as we are and communicate through people through their imperfections of a loving and just God. "This is what makes the Bible good news." We are in relationship with a God who's prepared to look ugly in the Old Testament so we would have a relationship with him. He's prepared to work through imperfect minds, memory, and sin allowing people to see him as an unjust God, so that those who can see through the Cross and its imperfections can see an awe-inspiring God. God is not a Zeus God, but a loving, caring, forgiving, amazing God. Understanding this, there is hope for all of us.

When we understand that in our imperfect state God will teach us and mentor us through imperfect people to bring about a much better person, then we can understand that this is why we trust the Bible and why we need mentoring in our lives. Christianity is not a spectator sport; it's about getting involved in the game. It's about getting bloody, getting involved in knowing God, and in co-working with God. This is the whole counsel of man to grow with God.

If you read the Bible for what it was meant for, which is to point you to Jesus Christ, on the cross, showing God's unfailing love, then I believe it is infallible. But if you're reading it for a science book, or history book with no imperfections, then I believe you will be disappointed. Anyone who says "how can you believe the Bible with all the errors?" reply to them, "they don't detract from the inspiration of the Bible; they contribute to the inspiration of the Bible."

God is acting towards us much like when I was reaching out to Marcus Gayle, a premiership soccer player.

I met Marcus at a church service in West London. I had no idea he was a premiership football player. His girlfriend Andrea introduced me to him. He was shy and not that easy to talk to. So, I had to find a way to connect with him. I asked him if he played soccer with his friends he said he did – every Thursday night at Shepherd's Bush. So, I asked him if I could join him. He smiled and said sure!

I turned up Thursday night at 7:30 in Shepherd's Bush. When I met everybody, there was a noticeable difference. I was the only pale skin one of everybody there. All of them made it obvious that they didn't want to get to know me. When it came to picking the players for the two teams, they made it even more obvious they didn't want to get to know me. They chose two captains and they started choosing the players. Marcus got picked first, obviously. They kept on choosing players until it finally got down to the last two players – me and another guy.

It was Marcus' captain who was to choose next. Marcus leaned over to him and pointing to me, said to pick him. You leave the poorest players to last, so, this certainly didn't make me feel included. But unbeknownst to them, I was an excellent soccer player. I played semi pro in Ireland.

The game began. We were playing 11 a side. Marcus was playing in the back. He had the ball, looked up and I raised my hand for him to pass it to me, which he did. I took the ball down with my chest, dribbled around two guys then looked up and took a shot at the goal. The next event must have been orchestrated by God because I had never experienced this in my life before. The goal post was not screwed together so that you could break them down and move them around.

My shot hit right at the top right-hand side of the post and cross bar. It shot the crossbar up and then the post and the crossbar came crashing down. The goalkeeper ran out for fear of his life!! As I was looking at this, my mind started to talk to me. It felt like everything was in slow motion. I said to myself "Did you see that? Wow I can't believe that just happened. This must be from God."

Then I realized that everyone was turning and looking at me. I felt like yelling "Oh yeah, now you know who I am! Yeah, respect me!! I do this every time I play. You think that dazzled you? You ain't seen nothing yet!" Of course, I didn't say that but everyone wanted to know me after that. But to me, what was more important than getting a little respect from others was that now Marcus felt a kindred spirit between us.

I think he must have felt like, man this guy came here to connect with me, put himself in an awkward position to know me, was disrespected, but never let it get to him. Marcus shared all this stuff later. We became great friends and helped a lot of people in life. This is what love and care does.

3) Foundation to Build Your Life Upon

Why believe in the Bible? Because it explains the greatest love story to ever enter our minds if we enter into solidarity with God. The Cross is God pouring his heart out to us. The next chapter will get into more of the details of the Cross.

I want to conclude this chapter by encouraging you to be mentored in your life. Once you understand that God is comfortable looking weak, working with imperfection, it takes away all fear of being trained and mentored. Mentorship speeds up the process of your growth.

Imperfect people can teach you when you bring the Holy Spirit into your life. There is no limit to what you can learn. Being mentored is a proactive decision on your part, not a coercive energy from God or his agents. Let me share one of my own experiences...

I joined an acting class to support a young man in his new venture. I felt obligated because he was in the Ministry where I was the preacher. I was thinking I would just turn up to show my face for 15 minutes, then leave. He had other ideas. Because I was the preacher and used to have a public presence, he thought that I would be comfortable being used as the ice breaker for his first class.

There were about 30 people in the class. He asked me if I would volunteer to support him in this exercise. I didn't want to be prudish, so I said of course. Then he asked me to step into the middle of the circle of people he had created with the class. Then he proceeded to teach about acting. He taught how you must start first by breaking down barriers to not limit yourself but to be free to express yourself – to embody the character or object you were portraying.

I was pretty comfortable in my own skin, so I wasn't too worried. But then he said, "Chris, I want you to act out a squeaking wheelbarrow." I thought he was joking at first. I began to laugh but he didn't laugh with me; he was serious. I thought, how in the world do you do that? Then I thought to myself, oh no, I am in trouble now...

I bent over with my hands to the ground (like down dog in Yoga) then walked around making a squeaking sound. I could see people chuckling to themselves. Then he said "Now, be a 6 month old screaming baby in his crib." I thought, OMG, what a mistake this was to support him!

Hoping this would end soon, I laid on my back with my arms and legs in the air screaming like I was having a tantrum. Next, he asked me to be a lemon. Yeah, I know. A what? A piece of fruit. How do you be a piece of fruit? In London, if you're a lemon, you're a fool or a turkey: a weak character guy. So, I started acting like a goofy fool.

Next was a rat, a snake and finally a ballet dancer!!

However embarrassing it may seem, a funny thing started to happen. I started to *not care anymore what people thought* in the room. The weirder it became, the more I was prepared to go there. It started opening my creative juices. As he was mentoring me, I began to appreciate what he was teaching me. I started getting in touch with things about myself that I never knew. I gained more wisdom in seeing how people limit themselves and how the social environment influences you.

That experience helped me be more dynamic in my public speaking. If I didn't get his guidance, I would have been a smaller self. Letting your limitations hinder you really robs you of life. Allowing yourself to be mentored opens the world to you in so many ways. God loves to work with imperfect people and circumstances. His glory is in looking weak. Paul says, *"When I am weak, then I am strong"* (2 Cor 12:10).

The pattern of this world is to hide who you really are – to appear like you have it all together. "Fake it til you make it" is a common teaching or understanding. The problem with that is you are creating another you. Your outward world is not aligning with your inner world. You have a mask on. Now you are training everyone to like or dislike the fake you, depending on what image you are betraying. Are you an outgoing, arrogant type of person or shy and insecure?

You have created a story of who you are not, by trying to live up to this image that you have made people believe. In time, you can't afford to be honest because it will be like a house of cards that comes crashing down. The Bible describes Satan as the father of lies (John 8:44). Father here is referring to being the best. Also, Satan manipulates a powerful delusion (2 Thess 2:11).

The pattern of this world is caught up in this make-believe world that is delusional. But God will not coerce you into doing his will. He lets you choose for yourself: your path of deliverance or destruction. He is always trying to help you choose the right path in subtle ways, through friends, whispers, reading, preaching, or kind acts of people. But you choose to believe in the delusion or not.

We live in a world of deception, believing and desiring things that are of less value for our soul. You get convinced that if you go with the majority, it must be right because everyone thinks so, thinks this feels real, right and normal. That is the deception, the path of destruction. But it is destroying your values and faith in humanity.

"Go in through the narrow gate; because broad and spacious is the road leading off into destruction, and many are the ones going in through it; whereas narrow is the gate and cramped the road leading off into life, and few are the ones finding it" (Matt 7:13,14).

Jesus says the path to deliverance or salvation of your soul is narrow. Only a few find it (Matt 7;15). To illustrate this, imagine life as a shop window display of clothing. You are viewing the clothes and desiring the expensive ones because you have disdain for the cheap clothing. What you don't realize is at night Satan went into the shop display and changed the price tags. He put expensive price tags on cheap clothing and cheap price tags on the expensive clothing. So, you are desiring the cheap clothes because you think they are the expensive ones. At the same time, you have no desire for the cheap clothes when in fact they are the expensive ones. Your perception is off because of the deception.

As you evaluate life, under the deception, what really looks good and worth sacrificing everything for are the cheap values and character of life, such as money, causal sex, a carefree life, drugs, quick fixes, no discipline in saying no to yourself, lying, pride, and/or drunkenness – all the really cheap things in life.

Whereas what looks foolish, a waste of time and effort and seems like the not important things in life are actually the expensive things in life like faith, commitment, self-control, honesty, a person of your word, humility, or a student of the spiritual world. These values really do give you life – life to the full, completely satisfying you. You have to see, feel and taste it to know how good and pleasing it is. Sadly, a lot of people have to be burned by the deception before they will make any change to grow a deeper understanding of what's important in life.

Why do I believe in the Bible? Because it opens a whole new world to me. It can be trusted as a source of guidance, wisdom directly from God. It teaches me to value what God values and to trust this standard or platform to build my life upon. To know God takes me as I am; I can trust in fallen men and women because God through the Holy Spirit is working with me to create the happy, secure, purposeful life I desire. Knowing God is comfortable looking weak is synonymous with when Paul says, "When I am weak, I am strong."

The Bible is divinely inspired; it communicates with me God moving in a relational way to mentor my life.

Praise God.

CHAPTER 6: CHRIST CONSCIOUSNESS THROUGH THE CROSS

Hebrew 1:3 says, "The Son is the radiance of God's glory and the exact representation of his being, sustaining all things by his powerful word. After he had provided purification for sins, he sat down at the right hand of the Majesty in heaven." This passage is saying that Jesus is the radiance of God's glory and the exact representation of God.

In the original Greek, the word translated from "exact" is hypostatic. Hypostatic means personal and exact. It means the very essence, the very being of God. It means the very nature of something. In other words, Jesus is God. Jesus is the hypostatic union of the divine and human. Jesus is the very nature of God. These two natures are united in one person in the God-man of Jesus. What makes God God is Jesus as the perfect revelation. As C.S. Lewis says, "Jesus is what the Father has to say to us." In other words, Jesus is the complete, total content and perfect vessel through which the Father speaks to us.

The story of the cross is the greatest love story there ever was. Through the sacrifice of Jesus Christ, God showed how much he loved us, his creation, human beings. He loved us so much that he surrendered and prepared himself to stoop down to our level. It would be as if one of us became an ant and then even a servant to the ants in comparison. And then, even allowing ourselves to be trampled on and killed.

When you apply the principles of Christ consciousness to all aspects of life, then not only are you living the teachings of Christ, but also, you can and will have a major impact on society for the betterment of the whole world. This is where the best leaders are created.

This chapter is about the power, the engine, the reason, and the spiritual fight that we all have against Satan and his entire wicked system of things. But it is also about what Christ consciousness is, how to apply it to ourselves, how to integrate it into what I call the 7 mountains of life – or the 7 pillars of life and how we need more leaders in the world who are true disciples of Christ. In the new testament, the word Christian is used 3 times and in the first century, "Christian" was actually a derogatory term. But the term "disciple of Christ" is used over 300 times. To get a better understanding of what it means to be Christian, the better term is disciple. Disciple means a student or follower of Jesus Christ – an imitator of Christ.

WHAT IS CHRIST CONSCIOUSNESS?

This incredible amount of love that God has for us is just one of the characteristics of Christ consciousness. But what does Christ consciousness mean? Christ consciousness means embracing the characteristics of Jesus in every aspect of your life, consistently. It's about being like Christ or having the Christ-like personality. It's about loving your enemies and praying for those who persecute you. It's about telling the truth in all things, even when it's hard or inconvenient, or even detrimental to your income or your safety, trusting in God to remedy the situation. It's about having integrity, standing up for what is right, being humble, and treating others the way that you want to be treated. But most importantly as already noted, it's about love – not the Hollywood romantic or the feel good, romanticized love – the love here is self-sacrifice. Self-sacrifice is described as agape love.

Agape is another form of Greco-Christian love. It is not to be confused with philautia which is self-love, or philia which is brotherly love. Agape love is total and absolute unconditional love – love for someone no matter the circumstance or the condition. That is the kind of love that God has for us.

Christ consciousness is about loving God, loving yourself, loving others, loving life, loving what you do, and striving to improve yourself in every way, all the time. But also, Christ consciousness is about forgiveness – forgiving yourself and others when you or others make mistakes.

It's also about not taking yourself too seriously in the sense of being humble, and yet always striving to do your best in everything that you do. Christ consciousness is about always having the mind of Christ so that you can make the right decisions in life, big or small. It's about helping your neighbor when you can, being generous to the needy when you are able, caring about others well-being and taking care of yourself.

In addition, it's about honoring your elders, seeking peace when others do not, turning your other cheek after getting slapped in the face, and yet, having the courage to stand up for what is right. Think of Christ's example when he opposed the money changers in the temple.

When you have Christ consciousness in your heart and mind, and you trust in God for everything to work out for you in every way, then you have true freedom – true spiritual freedom. You are then spiritually and financially free. How?

When you trust in God with all your heart and soul, you know that God will help you in every which way in life. You are free from worry. Free from doubt. Free from strife. Free from scarcity. Free mentally, emotionally, and spiritually. And when you are that free, God will reward your trust in Him, and the natural result is your own financial freedom too. You will become financially free because your faith will be strong that everything will always work out for you financially. You will be focused on excellence, whatever that is for you. And then through your excellence, faith and focus in whatever you desire to do for a living, you create value and strength of character that people will pay for.

The point is that just because you decide to become a disciple of Christ, it doesn't mean that everything that you ever wanted is going to magically be dropped into your lap. It takes inspired action effort along with having the foundation of Christ consciousness that is going to help you to create a successful life.

When you have that strong foundation of Christ consciousness, you have no doubt. You sleep well at night because you have a good conscience – Christ consciousness...

THE CROSS

The Cross represents God's ultimate love for us in sacrificing himself for His creation – us. Christ consciousness through the cross is about the art of allowing – allowing God's Holy Spirit to act in our lives and on our behalf. It's about surrender – surrendering our negative resistant vibration or negative feelings and allowing for God's grace to permeate our lives in every way.

The cross is about the vulnerability and the willingness of God to lower himself. It's about His attitude of, "I will lower myself to being a human in order to help you," even though he is omniscient, and the Almighty. As I mentioned already, it would be like if we decided to be an ant and allowed ourselves to be abused and beaten. That is how great God's love is for us.

But the cross is also about not having the victim mentality. Instead, it's about having a total belief in God. The cross is that level of belief – it contrasts the ugliness of humanity, yet the loving nature of God. In addition, it's about how we must take responsibility, and take action.

The Apostle Paul said to "fight the good fight," but it is not a physical fight – it is a spiritual one – an internal one – a conscious battle. It's a battle within our hearts and minds to do what is right, or to give in to doing what is wrong, upholding Christ's or God's values.

Unfortunately for us, the problem is that this is not God's world. This is Satan's world, as I will explain next.

SATAN IS THE RULER OF THIS WORLD

The cosmos has fallen into the hands of Satan. He is called "Archon" which basically means he is the CEO of this world! Our lives are in slavery to the spiritual forces of evil in the heavenly realms whether you are consciously aware of this or not. And this is happening right now!! What that means is, there is a spiritual war going on in the heavenly realms. The fight is to influence your thoughts and heart to a culture that honors those spiritual influences. "Archon" wants to perpetrate competition, hatred, lying, cheating, anger, and abuse. He is a proponent of lovers of power, value in cheap things, self-reliance, and arrogance...

When I say it's harder to change from a personal development point of view without God, what I mean is, there is a lack of understanding of metaphysics; there are great tools taught but there is a blinded effort to explain scientific reasons for change. The weakness of it all is that it dismisses man's weakness without God, trying to prop up victory without connecting to the source of our being.

Through the Cross of Jesus Christ, God enters into our weakness, our poor decision making or helpless state and shows us the paradox of the Cross – how it empowers us to change. Most Christian Churches have a completely different understanding of personal development or any other philosophy of change. The Christian concept of change is too generic and, in many ways, inept.

Church is a feel-good thing and unfortunately, it is not about the daily work in the marketplace. The church doesn't encourage the daily work, nor do they believe in it. They tend to believe that all their followers need to change are spiritual words of encouragement and nothing else. But to the contrary, you really must contemplate the glory of God, decide to become a disciple of Christ in every aspect of your life, and BE that person all the time – not just when it is convenient or easy.

The Biblical teaching of why it is difficult to change without God is because there is something bigger than humans going on. There is a Cosmic Battle going on that was settled at the epicenter, the Cross. We live in the fall-out from that.

Change is hard without God. The reason why is that everyone is in slavery to Satan as to what he wants and what he's doing. So, he's in the spiritual forces – he's in the cosmos. What Jesus did was strip Satan of all his powers.

Satan was an angel of light, and then fell from God. He was good but turned into evil. He created his own following. The epicenter of that was the cross. It benefited humans but also re-ordered the spiritual world too.

The result is that we live in a fallen world. We are not living in a perfect world. Before Noah's time, God said that every thought a man had was evil. To get rid of the evil, He created the flood.

God wants love on earth, but God gave mankind the free will to do what is right, or to do what is wrong. He knew it was risky because you must let people be themselves. You must allow people to show their own moral fiber. God has to allow his people to make their own choices, to stand up to wicked people. People wouldn't feel free if God intervened all the time. Not only that, but also, just like how the caterpillar needs the resistance of the shell, we need resistance to grow too.

The question is often asked, if there is a God, why does He allow for bad things to happen? The short answer is that He doesn't. The first thing to know is that God is not the source of bad things. James 1:13 says, "When tempted, no one should say, 'God is tempting me.' For God cannot be tempted by evil, nor does he tempt anyone." He gave us free will. Whatever you do with your life, God can't revoke that. Look at the example of Hitler. If all of us are to truly be free, we have to allow for people like Hitler who is the epitome of evil. At the other end of the spectrum to the good is Mother Theresa, or Gandhi. Within this spectrum, our freedom lies. Those are the definitions of how free we are with God.

The point is that God has got to allow us complete freedom. For God to allow us to have complete freedom, he's got to allow a Hitler to be free (as sad as that is, God is willing to take that risk). For a Mother Theresa or a Gandhi to live, through God's agape love for us, He also allows for anyone to have the freedom to be evil if they so choose. God has this undying unconditional love for us and between these spectrums of evil and goodness is our freedom. God allowing for this wide spectrum of behavior from man is part of the cost of being free.

This is why in this confused and messed up world, Jesus is the answer. He is the silver lining in the cloud.

God didn't intend on any of this happening. Natural disasters that kill people, or earthquakes, are not from God, but instead, because of the influence of Satan.

We live in a fallen world and cosmos. The evil and bad things that we see in the world are the results. God didn't create the animal world to be as violent as it is where they try to kill each other – that level of violence is the result of the fallen cosmos with Satan as the leader.

This also explains why governments oppress innocent people – it's because of the influence of Satan. Satan influences people to be wicked.

Most people see Satan as a red devil with a pitchfork. What they don't see is that lying, anger, deceit, and violence are all evil and a better representation of Satan. As stated, just like how the caterpillar needs the resistance of the shell, we need resistance to grow too. This is the very medicine that leads to wars and regimes rising up and killing innocent people – that culture, that influence from Satan fosters wicked men and women.

You may wonder, how does someone like Hitler become so evil? At one point in his life, he was a baby too, just like you and me. No doubt his parents loved him and whether they were great parents or not, as a young man, his nature started gravitating toward evil. Although no one can say for certainty exactly why Hitler hated the Jews, when he was young, he spent a lot of time in Vienna where antisemitism was very prevalent.

But also, around the time of World War I, the Jewish economic power was very strong in Germany – most banks, financial institutions and corporations were owned by Jews. This fact more than likely played a factor because Hitler believed that the Jews were conspiring together in order to take over all financial institutions worldwide. But also, Hitler believed that his race was superior to all others. In addition, he had an insatiable thirst for power which he thought would be thwarted by the Jews.

When he rose to power, he had a desire to fight for Germany. During World War I, his job was to run messages to the front line. In his book "Mein Kampf," he laid out his plan to make Germany a great nation. His attitude comes out in this. He wasn't a social charmer at all, but he had lots of opinions and solutions which helped him to galvanize the Nazi party which was really just a working-class party.

The point is that just how many people in the world do not recognize Satan as evil, no one recognized Hitler was evil at first either, until it was too late. He grew up and people tolerated him, but he had a wicked heart and no one dealt with it.

OUR MINDS AND HEARTS ARE THE BATTLEFIELD

Conversely from Satan, God wants to promote love, care, creativity, support, honesty, integrity, humility, joy, peace, patience, kindness, and faithfulness. The battle ground is your mind. Yes, you are free to choose how you interpret life, what values you live by. This is everyone's choice. But sadly, we tend to choose Satan's world. To live in the Spiritual realm, you have to focus and believe and trust in the unseen world.

This takes work, which is difficult for every human. Paul put it like this, *"The things I want to do, I don't do. And the things I hate to do, I keep on doing"* (Romans 7:18). Can you relate? It's a dilemma we all face whether we admit it or not. But we don't have to subject ourselves to this world. We've been given a choice at the Cross.

The point is that it's a choice. But it's not a choice that you make once in a while or once a week, rather, it's a daily choice – a choice in every moment. The choice we all have to make is whether or not we choose Godly thoughts, or the thoughts of Satan. That is the choice. Thought precedes action. And if the thoughts are impure, the actions will also be impure. But if they are thoughts that are in alignment with Christ consciousness, then the action will be beneficial to ourselves and to others.

In every moment and on every subject matter under the sun, we have the choice to think a negative thought, or a positive one. The battle is simple – choose the thoughts that are in alignment with Christ consciousness instead of ones that are not.

Again, our thoughts are powerful. Everything that God created started out as a thought as John 1:1 states where in the beginning, was the Word. To create or build anything, we first must have the thought of it, and then the vision before the first brick can be laid. The question then becomes, what sort of house are you building? Will it be one that can stand the test of time? Will it have a strong foundation on which to build? If it's centered around Jesus and the cross, it will be a strong foundation.

If you believe in God with all your heart, your foundation will be strong because all your thoughts will be in alignment with that belief. This is why belief is so important.

Understand that being authentic is your compass and that you're in control of your attitude. Your innate self, your natural state of being is that of love. You are not a mistake. You are perfectly made in the eyes of God. Your natural state of being is that of goodness. This is why your own internal emotional guidance system, in other words, your feelings, will tell you what is right and what is wrong in the moment. It's very simple. What feels good is usually right and is in alignment with Christ consciousness.

This is why prayer is so important. When you pray with a heart that trusts and *knows* you will be heard and answered, then there is no resistance to the prayer. But when a person prays from a feeling and a place of fear and trepidation, God cannot hear the prayer because it is fraught with doubt and worry.

This is why it is best to give prayer's of gratitude instead of prayers from a feeling place of desperation. When we beg God in prayer for anything, it's as if we are trying to manipulate Him – sort of like a nagging child who begs their parent. But prayers of thankfulness, appreciation and gratitude are in alignment with Christ consciousness and will not only be heard but rewarded with more of the same.

The battle is within your heart and mind and the choice is yours.

Paul described it this way; *"There is a veil, covering our mind."* You can't see solutions or a pathway to keeping a high level of motivation, to rise above the fray, with good respectable character that humanity admires. The mind is dull and powerless, subject to the lowest denominator – sin (sin simply means *"missing the mark"* as in, an archer missing the target) which means, missing the target on how to live! How to think in your mind! Listen to how Paul explains that without Jesus, our minds are blocked to understanding. 2 Cor 3: 8-18;

8) *"Will not the ministry of the Spirit be even more glorious?*

9) *If the ministry that brought condemnation was glorious, how much more glorious is the ministry that brings righteousness!*

10) *For what was glorious has no glory now in comparison with the surpassing glory.*

11) *And if what was transitory came with glory, how much greater is the glory of that which lasts!*

12) *Therefore, since we have such a hope, we are very bold.*

13) *We are not like Moses, who would put a veil over his face to prevent the Israelites from seeing the end of what was passing away.*

14) *But their minds were made dull, for to this day the same veil remains when the old covenant is read. It has not been removed, because only in Christ is it taken away.*

15) *Even to this day when Moses is read, a veil covers their hearts.*

16) *But whenever anyone turns to the Lord, the veil is taken away.*

17) *Now the Lord is the Spirit, and where the Spirit of the Lord is, there is freedom.*

18) *And we all, who with unveiled faces contemplate the Lord's glory, are being transformed into his image with ever-increasing glory, which comes from the Lord, who is the Spirit."*

Paul says the dulling veil that is over our minds has been lifted when we accept Jesus as our Lord. We can see the conflict and the glory of God. We understand the evil schemes of Satan. Why? Because the block is gone. How does that help us change? Well, when we turn to make Jesus lord, God gives us a helper, the Holy Spirit. He helps our motives to be pure and clean, entering a spiritual world of understanding. Do we have Satan accusing us? Yes, he never stops but now we understand where this energy is coming from. Here is what changed because of the Cross; here is what the Spirit does for us.

Trust God:

We trust God, knowing his ways are right and different to the world. The Holy Spirit speaks to us, in different ways. When you recognize his voice and practice trusting him, you know you are not alone. You carry yourself confidently waiting for his voice in everything.

The Fight is Not Physical but Spiritual:

Your Battle is not against flesh and blood but against the spiritual forces of evil, demonic powers. The battle is in our minds. The real estate is won there not by Zeus, but by Yahweh's Power (1 Cor 1:18) which is about surrender. The Holy Spirit speaks to us of this, reminding us of the cross.

God Doesn't Mind Looking Weak:

The cross is perplexing because the omnipotent God surrendered to humans allowing them to beat him to death. That doesn't look like a "Zeus God," Zeus being the Greek God of colossal strength and power. When

Yahweh gets big and powerful it looks like the Cross "beaten and surrendered." The world disdains that look of weakness and failure. However, the world doesn't understand how God releases unfathomable power with this surrender. This is the dichotomy of the cross and the Holy Spirit helps us to see through the cross and see a loving, caring God.

Comfortable Being Weak. Rom 7:18:

Paul articulates this so well. The behavior he wants to do, he can't do! But what he hates to do, this he keeps on doing. You learn to be happy with progress, not perfection. The Holy Spirit helps us to feel secure in our progress.

Living in Grace. Rom 8:1:

No condemnation: you now know you are not condemned; you are loved. You live in God's favor. God works for the good of those who love him. Nothing can separate you from the love of God. You are free from man's judgment and the spirit teaches us this.

The Renewing of Your Mind:

The paradox is contemplation; your work is to have faith, change your perspective, and trust in God. This makes you competent. Your value is in Yahweh, not yourself, allowing God to usher in change through the Holy Spirit.

We Have Authority:

We are restored to the authority that God gave us at the Garden of Eden. God gave authority to man to oversee the animal kingdom which is how we became the viceroys of the earth.

Change comes from contemplating the glory of God.

Spend time in your mind, seeing God and your life together. Bring unshakable Peace, Perspective and Confidence. This is what we gained at the cross. Your image of God defines everything: your attitude, your freedom, and your ethics. The Holy Spirit leads us here and shows us God.

The Love of God:

The intense love of God for us humans is seen at the cross. The enemy-loving, self-sacrificial, non-violent, loving God, is stooping down to our level almost like he is pressing his face against the Veneer of this world, showing us that he will do anything to reach out to us. He even allowed his Son to be brutally murdered at the cross by ruthless people! (The nature of humanity, without God.) The cross shows God moving towards us with love and sacrifice while humans move towards God with hatred and violence. That's the beauty and the ugliness of the cross. These epiphanies come from the Holy Spirit.

When the spirit gets you, God gets you! This fills us with joy and confidence. As the passages say, we become very bold – bold as lions.

Now with all this understanding, what then transpires in the mind?

God creates in us our own chapel; that is the imagination. Our minds can see the glory of God. The veil has been lifted from our minds. We have our sanctuary, our chapel, the imagination, our minds eye. At Romans 12: 1-3, Paul puts it this way;

"(1) Therefore, I urge you, brothers and sisters, in view of God's mercy, to offer your bodies as a living sacrifice, holy and pleasing to God—this is your true and proper worship.

(2) Do not conform to the pattern of this world but be transformed by the renewing of your mind. Then you will be able to test and approve what God's will is—his good, pleasing and perfect will. Humble Service in the Body of Christ.

(3) For by the grace given me I say to every one of you: Do not think of yourself more highly than you ought, but rather think of yourself with sober judgment, in accordance with the faith God has distributed to each of you."

THE CROSS IS THE POWER OF GOD

The cross is the bow that ties everything together. God gave birth to the human race and He, like any parent, would like to be loved back. He feels the same way towards us as we would with our own children. Any good parent would go to the extreme to help their child, even if it meant giving up their own life.

But a healthy minded parent knows that being an overly protective, helicopter parent is not good because just like with the butterfly, if you break the cocoon open too soon, it can't fly. The challenge for any parent is how much help do you give, and how much do you let them do on their own. There is no difference with God and us...

That is how much God loves us. He has a greater power than Zeus. Humans want God to wow them, but God wants to wow them through love, humility, and kindness. That is who God is, and because we were made in the image of God, that is who you and I are naturally too. You are secure and confident as a human being.

But most of the world is filled with people who lie, cheat, steal and who will resort to violence to settle any matter. In general, today, humanity without God is like in the days of Noah when *"every thought of a man is evil."* But through the cross, God showed us how to be a spiritual person through Christ consciousness.

Christ consciousness is the cross. Jesus knew the nature of man well enough to know that they were going to kill him – but he stayed in the zone of humility and love. He loved his enemies regardless of what they did to him. And he sacrificed Himself for all of us.

Christ consciousness through the cross is enemy loving, sacrificial, non-violent, surrendering to God. When you embrace Christ consciousness for yourself, it becomes the trigger that releases the power of God by its nature. The power of the cross or Christ consciousness is like spinach for Popeye. It is there for you at any moment to empower you to do the right thing. The result is not like Popeye with immediate power. Long lasting character is forged over time and character overcomes resistance like Popeye. Through the cross, you get long-lasting strength of character.

The cross equips you with the right attitude, the confidence to know that love, joy, peace, humility and trusting in God is the best way to live. Through the cross, you understand why man needed saving and why Jesus came down to show that even in this fallen world you can learn to forgive people, etc.

The nature of God is a way – he will show you the more excellent way to live. You've got to be committed to that. In the cosmic forces in the spiritual 4th dimension, we can overcome anything if we eat the spinach of the cross.

Colossians 1:13 says that we were saved "from the power of darkness and transferred... into the kingdom of his beloved Son." All who accept this truth are thereby reinstated to the original position and responsibility of stewards of the creation that God had always intended for us. We have been liberated from the destructive and tyrannical ruler, Satan, after Jesus retook his rightful position on his throne. The main reason why Jesus appeared was to "destroy the one who has power of death, that is, the devil" (Heb 2:13).

This is the power of a Christian life. The power to change! How? By contemplating the glory of God, not by effort or performance but by allowing your mind to be open to seeing God and life differently. This can come across as weak nonsense because to change involves effort. Looking at it from a life without Jesus, yes, it appears that way. It is hard to change, Why? We have built a framework of thoughts and attitudes from childhood that we are comfortable with and have faith in. We have learned to live life at this level. The bad attitudes, the stress, the scarcity, the struggle, we are familiar with. We have come to accept this, as life. To change is disruptive! You may or may not like this process! It feels soft, simple, and purposeless. The doubt sets in and you may start to ask yourself, "Can I really do this? Can I sustain change? Can I keep this up?"

This is the crucible of change. What is the hard part to understand? That you do nothing! Did I say "You do nothing?" Yes. You must surrender and allow God time and space to enter your mind's thoughts, hunches, and coincidences. Out of nothing comes guidance; this is God moving towards You. Like a magnet, perspective is drawn to You. This is surrender. This is the cross like attitude Jesus came to teach us to trust in! So, tackling life is to *contemplate the glory of God* and he will lead you to where you want to go! Yes, when you believe what God did for you at the cross, You can let go and let God.

Our Competence is in God, Not Us! (2 Cor 3)

What does contemplate the glory of God really mean? Does it mean that we just sit there like a Buddha, doing nothing and God changes us? No. You enter into an "active meditation." You go about your life normally, but your antennas are up. God will show you Natural Laws and Spiritual Laws and you begin to see how they work. You develop confidence in trusting them.

The key to change is motivation. What creates motivation? Belief that you are the creator of your life – not coming from a competitive space, but from a creative space. Competition comes layered with the feeling of scarcity, performance, and anxiety. We live with the idea of "the pie" concept which is that there isn't enough pie to go around for everyone, so we are all living in scarcity. There is only one pie and only so much that goes around! But that is not God's belief. That is fearful man's belief.

As a result, this creates a spirit of "time is of the essence; work harder, perform or get out of the way...." This is the stress filled world we live in. Some rise to this but most are crushed by it. But when you believe God loves you, as seen at the cross, your mind is open. You see how God has set up proven scientific laws that work when honored, like gravity, radio waves, buoyancy, splitting of the atom, aerodynamics, etc.

We see this in everyday life. God shows us through physical laws (that we can see) that there are spiritual laws at work too (that we can't see). But they work just the same. He teaches us through physical law that there are spiritual laws. There are spiritual laws like love, giving, trusting, and faith. This is living a spiritual life. It creates a harmonious culture. These laws are freely chosen by anyone when you realize that God set them up. You choose confidently with faith. This takes an act of faith knowing that God has set this up.

Everything that has been created in this world came from honoring these principles. Coming from the creative world, knowing God loves and you know "God works for the good of those who love him," you begin to understand that God will bring life to your thoughts. You want to spend more time thinking because you know God will help you to percolate more ideas. You don't have to perform, it's your idea! You are working with your creator – working with God.

On your "active meditation" schedule, opening your mind to God, you will begin to see and understand things while you are working. Coming from the creative space, you will find that there is no pie! Abundance abounds everywhere. God is the source of everything. You are not competing with anyone. Your ideas are your ideas with God. He will take you where you want to go. So, doing a good day's work is good enough. You don't have to do more. In your leisure time, contemplate and let God work with you while trusting in God, knowing he knows what's best, and that his timing is perfect. When you live from the creative world with God, you are confident, not in you but in God! You are not in a hurry. You're peaceful, knowing that God is working with you.

The power is in the cross and it turns everything upside down.

So many Christians see the cross as a piece of art: a statue, a piece of jewelry. Then they acknowledge that Jesus died for them which is true. It's followed by a fleeting thought "Thank you God, for dying and saving my soul." That is it!! That's their understanding of the cross. Yet there is so much more going on. At 1 Corinthians 2:2,

SPIRITUALLY AND FINANCIALLY FREE

Paul says *"I know nothing but Jesus Christ and him Crucified."*

What is going on here? Such different perspectives. Paul is saying *"Everything I see in life, I view through the lens of Jesus Christ and him crucified."* He didn't rely on his talent, his knowledge, or his intelligence (he was a genius). He looked at the cross with a different perspective.

He saw God stooping down to our level, allowing humans to kill him so that we understand that God loves us! God knows we need help. We live in Satan's domain, the earth, which is full of legalism, hatred, performance, a competitive world, a culture of stress, scarcity, worry, hardship, anger, and pain. All because Satan, or Archon (CEO) is harsh who knows nothing about love. God moves toward us through the cross stooping down to our level to show us a more excellent way to live. By this act of self-sacrifice, this enemy-loving, non-violent God shows us an image of Jesus dying on the cross for others. He is showing us dying to our selfish desires as Jesus did on the cross. This dresses you with an attitude of love, giving, kindness, encouragement, joy, peace, gentleness and faithfulness. He teaches us how to combat this world by understanding a self-sacrificial, non-violent enemy-loving God shown at the cross when we allow God to give us a more visual image of that!! Satan and his captains have no idea how to relate to or deal with this attitude. They don't understand LOVE. This is how glorious our God is: illuminated at The Cross.

THE WEAPONS WE FIGHT WITH

Since the battle is with our hearts and minds, what do we fight with?

Our weapons are not made of steel and gun powder. Our weapons are completely different. The weapon of choice from the Christ consciousness point of view is with surrender. The way we fight is by living a life of humility, kindness, goodness, and faithfulness. It's by contemplating the glory of God and never wavering from Christ consciousness in all our thoughts, deeds and actions. Of course, none of us are perfect and that is why we need forgiveness, but if we constantly strive to be better than we were before, we are on the right path of righteousness.

Righteousness is simply choosing the right path – the right way to be – the right way to love, and the right way to live.

Surrendering is the same thing as the art of allowing. The art of allowing is trusting in God so much so that you never offer up thoughts of negative resistance such as doubt, fear, worry, strife, anger, rage, or revenge. But again, none of us are perfect and we all eventually give into resistance. It's not about whether or not you will have resistant thoughts – it's about how quickly you can let the resistance go.

Allowing is trusting in God that no matter what is going on in your life in any aspect of it, things are going to get better. It's about forgiving others, not entertaining lower vibrational thoughts and feelings, and choosing to look at the bright side of life no matter what.

These higher vibration weapons of choice will allow you to live a happier, longer, and more fulfilled life than anyone who is stuck in Satan's wicked world.

When you use the weapons of Christ consciousness, you have a certain spirituality about you. Nothing can deter you from your convictions and path because you have built a foundation upon which to create the life that you genuinely want.

VICTORY: WE ARE MORE THAN CONQUERORS

We are more than conquerors. We are influencers who at any aspect of society can take over and change it. We must see ourselves in this light because if not, Satan's world is simply going to get more and more out of control.

This is where the churches are dropping the ball when it comes to leadership. They are allowing things to happen without much concern. The result is that more and more our freedoms are being taken away from us.

God needs people in the 7 mountains of life. There are serious concerns in the political arena about stamping out our freedom. This is why we need men and women who can handle that in a Christ consciousness, Godly manner. We can no longer just play it safe and let others take over and take charge. But we must allow God to open the doors for us so that we can do our part.

Chapter 6: Christ Consciousness Through the Cross

But it's not easy to step up to the plate of life! This is an in-depth understanding of why we have the confidence to change. I am looking at it from a balanced life, a long-term view with consistent healthy motivation.

What are the challenges I see for change? Change stems from motivation. I am approaching this from a spiritual point of view. To those who have doubts about the spiritual world, I am not saying you can't change but I am saying it is harder. Some of the motives to change are:

Value - Your life has to mean something.

Vision - You want to see where you're going.

Freedom - You want to design your life on your own canvas.

Family - Create culture that means something to You.

Authenticity - Be honest with yourself. Not conditioned by other people.

Philosophy - Your personal Code you live by.

The victory that Christ won on the cross is more substantial than Christ simply dying for us. The main point is that the cross represents ousting Satan as ruler and instead re-establishing Jesus as the one and only loving ruler. This is why we can state with absolute certainty that Christ now reigns and is far more powerful than any demonic being. After all, the power of Satan and his demons was stripped away after the sacrifice of Jesus.

In essence, because Jesus was victorious, we are saved. This is significant for me personally because it helps me to believe my work has authority.

How does that practically affect us today? How does that help us change today? This seems more like "Star Wars" than real life. It seems like "Star Wars" because of how our world dismisses the Spiritual conflict as childish, not real, like Disney world – something made up or a fantasy world of make believe. This affects our minds and how we think. The mind becomes the place to fight, especially for Christians. We feel like we are swimming up stream with our thoughts and what we fight to live for.

But understand this; it is a fight worth fighting. As quoted earlier, Paul says, *"Fight the good Fight."* So how do we have an advantage as Christians to make changes in our minds?

Satan feeds us two streams of thought in everyday occurrences. One is condemning thoughts, such as, you're at fault, or you do this all the time. Zac 3:1 says, *"Satan stands accusing us all day long."* That's a negative feed every hour of the day. The second stream of thought is that he coaches us to be arrogant, aloft, and to rise above the issues at hand, encouraging us to not take responsibility and to tell ourselves "Let others deal with it! This is below my pay grade."

CAPTAIN OF YOUR OWN SHIP

I was in the ministry and circumstances led me to believe I should look for something else. While I was doing my job as a minister, I was looking for an opportunity to create financial freedom so that I could serve the people from a place where my job didn't depend upon it. At the

Chapter 6: Christ Consciousness Through the Cross

time, I was living in Atlanta Georgia. I grew up most of my life in London. I came up with an idea to develop a property developing company in London which I did. It was called "Atlantic Properties."

I had a general idea of what I was going to do, and I was familiar with doing things from a distance because I was training ministers in different countries. I had no money, but I did have an idea. I tried 15 properties in West London to see if I could accomplish this. I had architects and builders checking out these properties to see if I could execute my idea.

But things weren't going well and soon after, I found myself in the back of a car crying my eyes out because I'd given up my job, had three sons that I needed to feed and mentor, a mortgage to pay and a wife to support. I stepped out on faith in this venture but found myself scared to death. "I've made a mistake, I've made a mistake!" I kept telling myself. But then, I found my peace and I remained faithful to my vision and my dream.

As I was lying in the back of this car, I came up with the question of what about South East London? So, I jumped on a scooter and drove all around South East London looking for property. After a little while of searching, I came across a property that had already had planning permits, which was a godsend. Planning permission generally takes three months to get the OK or they could extend it for six months depending on what you're asking for. I couldn't afford to wait for more than three months. This was perfect for me.

As I started the build with a team of construction guys, it was during the summertime and we were having a blast. The neighborhood became very friendly towards me, especially the neighbor across the road. His name was Matt. He asked me would I be interested in buying his house. I said yes because it was an end semi-detached house. It had a significant patch of land beside it that was a gold mine in urban London. I asked him what he was going to do with his money. He said he and his wife were going to buy an RV and drive around Europe, put the rest of the money in a credit saving account that pays 5% and they would live off of that! I asked, "Would you be interested in putting $100k into my company and I would give them 10%?" He said he would talk to his wife and let me know.

He came back the next day and said yes, they would do that even when the Realtor during the close of escrow was telling them that it was a mistake. Matt and his wife Margret, said no, we know Chris and trust him. As a result of that, I was able to get planning for eight apartments between the house and the land. So, having nothing, I found seed money to start my company and it went from zero to $3 million worth in value in two years. I was looking for an idea to fill my heart's desire, trusting that God would come through if I was loyal to my vision in my imagination. God did come through.

Using your mind and imagination, trusting God and his laws, you can create the life that you want to create. This is the way God intended for us to live. We are the captains of our own ship, charting through waters that we desire to the destination of our dreams.

THE 7 MOUNTAINS OF LIFE

These 7 mountains are all the different aspects of life and culture, namely: family, church, government, media, the arts, education, and business.

What does Christ consciousness through the cross look like when you apply it practically to the marketplace of the 7 mountains of life?

Let's first look at the media as a good example. What if you were a journalist and your manager asked you to lie about a story to cover something up? Would you compromise your integrity? What would Christ have said or done? Why wouldn't you tell the truth? Would it be because of the fear of losing your job? But couldn't you get a better job if you put your faith in God?

If you are asked to lie on the job, is your integrity worth it? Is your relationship with God worth it? This is applying Christ consciousness to the cross.

Or let's say that you are in education as a schoolteacher. Education, unfortunately, has recently been heavily influenced by nefarious entities who wish to harm the family unit and all that is pure, whole and good about children. Some school efforts are out there to force a 4-year-old child to identify as one gender or the other! That is nothing short of child abuse. What would you do as teacher and a disciple of Christ? Would you allow it? Or would you stand up against the teachers union?

Would you attempt to stop the insanity? Or would you step aside and go along with it?

This is what it means to adorn Christ's personality – Christ consciousness through the cross.

Or, to highlight the business mountain, what if you were a banker? And what if you came across shady banking business practices that your bank was involved in? Would you sweep it under the rug and just go along with it? Or would you tell your boss and trust that if you lost your job, that God would supply you with something even better? If you were in the banking industry, you wouldn't compromise your integrity; you would give the best service that you could and if you lost your job, you would trust in God to replace it with something better or that He would remove the people who were chastising you.

The point is that if you are a disciple of Christ, you would apply Christ's principles and teachings in all areas of your life, always. You wouldn't be a part-time, Sunday attending Christian, but instead, a real, true, disciple of Christ. Luke 9:23 explains what a disciple is. It says, *"Then he said to them all: 'Whoever wants to be my disciple must deny themselves and take up their cross daily and follow me.'"*

What Jesus is saying here is that anyone who wants to become a disciple of Christ must learn to say no to yourself. You must say "no" to wicked inclinations and you must be willing to "die" to yourself every day – to pick up your cross and follow Jesus.

Chapter 6: Christ Consciousness Through the Cross

The cross is the attitude of trust in God – it's complete faith to be resurrected in our lives on a daily basis. It's the faith that if we personally died on the cross ourselves in standing up for what is right, that God would resurrect us just like Jesus.

And what about the government mountain? Much of the world is in disarray because of corrupt, greedy politicians who care not about the people but instead, about power and their own pocketbook. What if you were working in some form of government and you saw something that was really wrong, and which hurt others? Would you go along with the politics of it and play the political game of turning a blind eye? Or would you do the right thing?

Again, Paul says at 1 Cor 2:2 *"For I resolved to know nothing while I was with you except Jesus Christ and him crucified."* Imagine what it would have looked like if Paul was a politician. Do you think that he would have just gone along with the political game like all the others?

Think of what the world would be like if ALL politicians applied the principles of Christ and implemented Christ consciousness in all their efforts! Our entire planet would be a much safer, sane, and abundant world.

DREAM BIGGER AND BE BIGGER

When you look at the 7 mountains of life, it allows you to evaluate your own life. Churches don't do that. They don't really encourage their followers to dream bigger and to be bigger. They don't get into how to improve the world really. Most seem to encourage mediocrity over accomplishment and success in life, and it really has had a detrimental effect on all of us because we find ourselves under the constant suppression and even oppression by Satan's wicked world.

This is why the Christian religion, even though it is the largest religion on planet earth, has lost its influence. Church leaders are not leading at a time when now, more than ever, we need strong disciples of Christ to lead us out of the problems that we have today.

Whether you are the leader of a political party, or the leader of a major corporation, when it has at the core of its leadership the characteristics of Christ consciousness, it will benefit everyone in some way, even if it is small. If we had men and women of character in these higher positions, it would bring people together, help them feel safe and benefit the whole world.

All you have to do is to dream bigger and be bigger...

But it is no easy task. 1 Cor 1:18 says, *"The cross looks foolish to those who are perishing – but to us who are being saved, it is the power of God."* Anyone picking up the cross and leading their lives by it will be ridiculed and made to look foolish to the world. That is happening now more than ever. But we must dawn the Christ consciousness characteristic of courage in everything that we do, knowing full well that God will help and even save us if necessary.

Again, Luke 9:23 says, *"Lift up your cross daily and follow me."* Notice that it says daily, not weekly. That sets a tone for the next verse. *"If you want to save your life, you will lose your life. And if you want to lose your life, you will save it."* In other words, if you give up your worry about your own life and trust in God to carry you through any challenge in any aspect of your life, then you will save your life, not lose it. If you no longer surrender to doubt, fear and worry through the Christ consciousness of the cross, you will save your life. It will open your life to a whole new spiritual world.

Time is of the essence. Our world has suffered greatly because there are not enough disciples of Christ taking the lead. Luke 9:60 says, *"Let the dead bury their own dead, but you go and proclaim the kingdom of God."* Jesus was talking about priority here. We need to make God and Christ consciousness our priority so that we can not only set the example for others, but also so that we can lead more effectively. Concern yourself only with God's business and don't get distracted by the world.

The time is now.

Satan has a powerful delusion – Satan wants to delude us into believing that if we stand up for what is right, our lives will be over. But if you have to stand up for what is right on the job, they can fire you but not take your life. That's the heart of a disciple. That is what we are lacking in all of these 7 mountains or areas of life.

Judas ended up hanging himself after accepting 30 pieces of silver for betraying Jesus. Many of us, if not careful, can fall under Satan's delusion and sadly be like Judas, denying Christ and his value. The point is that we are not people of faith just because we go to church on

Sundays. A disciple is someone who brings Jesus to the marketplace and not just when he goes to church on Sunday.

But the cross cultivates the world or the culture that God wants us to live in – a world of peace, a world that unites families, a healthier society in every way. Even though it may be hard at first, as more and more disciples of Christ become leaders, if we live with Christ consciousness through the cross, we will impact the 7 mountains of culture.

Chapter 7: Covenant Leadership

Covenant is a commitment regardless of the circumstances – retaining covenantal trust in one's covenant partner in the face of uncertainty. It is like "unconditional love" where a person loves another regardless of conditions. A covenant is a binding agreement between two parties of loyalty and support for one another.

Covenant leadership then, is really about being the type of leader who is committed to both God and to those who are led.

But before we discuss leadership, let's discuss the state of mind that is necessary to have first.

How Gratitude Strengthens Your Relationship with God

Now that you understand what God has done for you and how much he loves you, you should be full of gratitude and love. And because you were made in God's image, you know you are Love too. And now that you know who God is and who you really are, you know you can build your life on a solid foundation.

When you realize God's love, it's as if the scales which blinded you before fell from your eyes. You not only see how much God loves you, but also how much God has set things up for you to co-work with you to build within you a strong desire to have a lasting relationship with God. And once you have that solid, strong relationship with God, you can use it to build a solid foundation for all aspects of your life.

Once you can grasp and understand the prior chapters, you can see the good in all of life. God has set up natural metaphysical laws that if we harmonize our spirit with, will allow us to play our own music, co-working with God.

The key is to have gratitude for all of life – the ups, the downs, the good, and the not so good. For example, when a cherished relationship ends, when you have the strength of God with you, you will be able to be grateful for the relationship regardless of why it ended. Another example is money. If you suddenly find yourself in financial trouble, you can still find a way to be grateful for what you do have.

THE POWER OF GRATITUDE

Your own music is your own true desires in life. Your own music can only be heard by you. Only you know when you are being your true authentic self, or not. This is why we spent an entire chapter on how to be authentic.

It is imperative that you be true to yourself first because if you *try* to be grateful but you don't actually *feel* it, you won't attract or receive what it is that you want. In other words, it won't do you any good to feel grateful if it is not authentic.

The best way to manifest what you want is to first get into harmony with God. What this means is that you not only understand that it's a two-way street with God, of giving and receiving, but also, you are a vibrational match to the essence of God. In other words, you are in total harmony in spirit.

When you bathe yourself in the feeling of gratitude on a continual basis, you then create the harmonious relationship with God.

To further develop a harmonious relationship with God, all you have to do is to fully believe in Him as God. Next, you understand and believe that He is the giver of all that you desire. And finally, you embellish the feeling of gratitude, not because of the things that God gives you, but because you know that feeling gratitude is the best way to *BE*, regardless of your circumstances in life. This gratitude doesn't require you to have to wait for what it is that you want, but rather, it is a way of *being,* of human-being – the act of feeling and being grateful for the simplest and the smallest things in life.

It is not about waiting around for God to deliver what it is that you want so that you can then be grateful. It's about being grateful for life itself and everything that you have in your life *now,* no matter what your current condition is. It's about finding a way to be grateful for a fish head in a bowl of water, and truly feeling the appreciation.

When a person isn't grateful for what they have in their life, they lack faith. They are never quite satisfied with what they have and are always looking for something to come along before they can feel grateful. Rarely does it ever come, however, because life and natural laws do not reward those who are never satisfied with what is directly in front of them.

When a person doesn't give God credit for the gift received, they cut ties with Him. Their future abundance is cut short. They quickly dismiss what was given and don't attribute it to God's act of grace. This leads to a disharmonious relationship with God, and therefore a disparaging life of struggle, strife and a focus on lack instead of abundance.

It should be clear that the person who is grateful to God is closer to Him, and the more that they shall receive. This is why those who have a harmonious relationship with God are generally happier than those who do not. And this explains why many rich and famous celebrities are usually not happy, no matter how rich or famous they are.

Furthermore, it only makes sense that the more grateful that we are to God, not only will we receive what we desire quicker, but also, more will come to us.

The longer that you can stay in that feeling of gratefulness and appreciation, the more God's abundance will come to you. The reason simply is that the mental attitude of gratitude draws the mind into closer touch with the source from which the blessings come. It's really more of a choice than a predicted outcome. You can simply choose to focus on the things that you are grateful for at any time that you want in order to manifest the feeling of appreciation.

The number of things that you can be thankful for are endless. Anyone can stir within their heart the feeling of being grateful and appreciative. You can be thankful for the sun rise, the sunset, the morning's fresh air, the birds, the trees, water or having a roof over your head. You can be thankful for the bed you lay in at night, or the new pillow that feels so good to you. Or you could be thankful that we have a beautiful earth with so much to see and explore. The things that we can be grateful for are bountiful and may have nothing to do with your earthly possessions, but instead, for all that we normally take for granted, such as fresh air, a wonderful friendship, our family and friends, or a walk on the beach.

What you now have and possess is because you have obeyed the law of gratitude. It's almost as if you can pave the way for more abundance to come to you, the more grateful and appreciative you are. In addition, gratitude will keep you in close harmony with creative thought and prevent you from falling into competitive thought.

When you practice the art of being grateful and appreciative, you will find more and more things to be grateful for. That's the way that it works. If you aren't used to being grateful on purpose, it may seem fake to you. And although feeling the genuine feeling of appreciation is the only way to attract more things to be grateful for, it doesn't hurt to prime the pumps of that feeling with thoughts that don't quite yet feel genuine. In other words, it's okay, at first, to "fake it til you make it," but realize that if you never really feel the feeling, nothing will change.

The interesting thing with feeling gratitude to God regardless of your circumstance is that it implicitly includes the limitless, fully abundant mindset. God is infinite. His abundance is infinite. His power is infinite. And He cares deeply about you, your loved ones, and his co-creative relationship with you. This is why you don't have to worry about anything. When you fully trust in God, you then have nothing to worry about. Worry brings on fear and scarcity, which is the opposite of having a harmonious relationship with God. God cares for those who have faith in Him to provide the abundance that they seek.

THE LAW OF GRATITUDE

The Law of Gratitude works whether you believe in it or not. Isaac Newton's third law is that for every action, there is an equal and opposite reaction. Whenever one body exerts a force on another, the second body exerts an equal and opposite force on the first body. The same can be said of the Law of Gratitude. The Law of Gratitude is the concept that action and reaction are equal because you will receive from God the equal amount that you are grateful for.

When you are grateful for everything, more of what you want will come to you. James 4:8 says, "Draw near to God, and He will draw near to you." The more praise you give to God and the more grateful you are to Him, then the more you will be liberated.

Jesus was always grateful and showered praise on God whenever he could. He said *"I praise You, Father, because you have hidden these...."* (Matt 11:25; Luke 10:21). He gave thanks *before* feeding 5,000 (Jn 6:11), *before* raising Lazarus (Jn 11:41), and *before* the Last Supper (Luke 22: 17). Jesus gave thanks a lot. When you are not grateful for what you have, you diminish your power. The inverse is true too. The more grateful you are, the more powerful you become.

This is why praying from a thankful heart is much better than praying from a lackful, desperate heart. When you thank God for all that is and for everything in your life from a humble, meek and mild position, God will fill your cup to the full. But when you pray from the perspective of scarcity, whining, pleading, and asking, you offer up resistance in your prayers, thereby not only canceling out what it is that you seek, but also jeopardizing what you already have.

When a person is not grateful, it becomes almost impossible to be positive – a positive attitude and gratitude go hand-in-hand. Not only that, but when you are not grateful, it is nearly impossible to pray and have it be productive.

When you get too focused on the current conditions in your life from a negative perspective, you lose any momentum that being grateful gave you. When you focus on the difficulties in your life, regaining a positive attitude gets even harder. Your subconscious mind begins to believe that your lot in life is permanent, unchangeable, and it will seek to continue to keep it that way. Then, just like a vicious cycle, you convey these thoughts to God, thereby inviting more of what you don't want into your reality.

When you allow yourself to constantly think about inferior things, you set yourself up to attract inferior things. But if you purposely think about superior things, you will attract those instead. Where you choose to put the focus of your mind makes all the difference in the world.

All of us have the power within us to create what we want by focus and attention. We are powerful, creative, physical beings who can create that which we think about. The grateful mind will receive the best when it focuses on the best.

From Gratitude Comes Faith

Gratitude and positive expectation manifests into faith. With strong faith, you are able to be grateful during any and all circumstances.

When you have gratitude in your heart, you do not focus on the lack in your life. You do not regret the past or worry about the future. When you are in the state of mind of gratitude and appreciation, you do not invite doubt to enter and spoil the feeling. Instead, you have a strong faith that your future will be even brighter than your present circumstance.

BE GRATEFUL FOR EVERYTHING

You may think, "How can I be grateful for everything? How can I be grateful for corrupt leaders, corporations, or politicians? Or for a failed economy and all of the injustices in the world?"

It is very tempting to complain about corrupt politicians, the wealthy and those of influence, but they have very little to do with your own reality and your own ability to create abundance in your life. And even though they are corrupt, they have helped to create a system in which you can attract unlimited abundance. Even the most corrupt political system usually has created an economic system in which you can thrive. In other words, if anarchy ruled, you wouldn't have a chance to thrive in life. Jesus explains this at Mark 12:17, where he said, "Give back to Caesar what is Caesar's and to God what is God's."

This takes focus and work to frame these things. 2 Cor. 10:5 says, *"Take captive of every thought."* As a disciple of Christ, do not buy into the negativity that surrounds us. The way to differentiate negative thinking versus positive thinking is that the cross is loving and kind. It's done with a spirit of kindness and gentleness.

BEING GRATEFUL EVEN FOR PAIN

I have experienced learning how to be grateful for even the painful things in my own life, in a profound way. My youngest son Joshua was in a lot of pain, but he wasn't even conscious of it and neither was I, at first. He was completely shut down in his emotions. At 15, he lost his whole family. Let me explain...

We were a family of five. Once the divorce occurred, his two older brothers left; one went to college, the other went to live on his own. I was so focused regarding my own pain that I abandoned him and left for California. In a sense, his mother abandoned him too because she was consumed with making a livelihood, once she was on her own. She was working from 7 am until 7 pm, 6 days a week, so she rarely had any time for Joshua.

He remembers our family as happy, loving, joyful and full of energy. Now, there was only silence, loneliness, no father, no brothers, and a limited time with his mother. Joshua was left to fend for himself. He started missing high school frequently, hung out with his buddies who became his family, and started smoking pot and getting drunk. There was no parenting or supervision in his life. In time, Joshua felt angry and distant from me. He felt like there was no point in talking on the phone. He wanted me to be there. But he was hurt because I abandoned him, and rightfully so. He wouldn't respond to my calls. We didn't talk for almost a year. I was so hurt back then; I didn't understand his pain!

But then when I went through "grief recovery" for myself, I finally started to understand Joshua's pain. He was just functioning, not living and not excited about his life. He lost his motivation to be excellent.

When I realized what had happened to Joshua, I started to cry and pray that God would give me back the years lost with Joshua during his high school years. I prayed this prayer for seven years. I began to pray for *"the year of the Locust"* (Joel 2:25) where God told his people that he would replace the harvest that was eaten by the Locust. He said, *"I will give it back to you"* and for me too, He did!!

Through my pain I started to be grateful for the lessons I was learning in life and for how God was there through all my poignant painful moments in life. He wasn't going to coerce me into loving him, but when I was ready to reach out for him, he was there. I started to fix my mind on God and his wonderful counselor by harmonizing myself with his Spirit, seeing the good in life and knowing that God works for the good of those who love him.

It was during this time of me feeling gratitude that suddenly, out of the blue, drunk, Joshua called me at 2 am. He said, "Dad, I miss you and want to reconcile our relationship. I am a complete mess. I've been fired from my job. I am lying to my family. I told mom and my brothers that I was working on Mother's Day and they came to my restaurant to surprise me, but I was not there – I was out with my friends getting drunk... Can you bring me out to California for a week?" Immediately, I said, yes!

In two days, he was here. A week later, he decided that he never wanted to go back to Atlanta, Georgia. He loves California and plans to spend the rest of his life there. He felt like he had a new start in life, and he never looked back. Now, he is going back to college. He has built out a dream for himself. As far as I am concerned, I feel like I am restored as a dad.

I am so happy in life with him. We play pool together several times a week. We are very close. One of his bucket list things to do was to snow ski. So, I took him to "Big Bear" in California before we were to go to Aspens.

After all this restoration of my relationship with Joshua, I realized that God had given me back the years I lost with Joshua. Now, I am so grateful for "the year of the Locust." The lesson to learn here is to fill your life with gratitude. When you feel gratitude in your heart for a sustained amount of time, God will give you more things to be grateful for...

The story of Keanu Reeves is a good one to show how being grateful even when things go wrong is the best way to go. His life before the theater might surprise you. He was abandoned by his father at 3-years-old and grew up with 3 different stepfathers. Also, he is afflicted with dyslexia. Before he decided to get into acting, he wanted to become a hockey player, but he had a serious accident that kept him from ever playing again.

Keanu had many other serious setbacks in his life. For example, his sister battled leukemia, his best friend River Phoenix died of an overdose, his wife died in a car accident, and his daughter died at birth.

But even though Keanu had many setbacks, he never let tragedy get him so down to keep himself from helping others who were in need. He is known for donating huge amounts of money to hospitals. One of the stories goes that while they were filming "The Lake House," he overheard two assistants talking about their problems. One of them said that she was about to lose her house if she didn't quickly come up with $20,000. After hearing this, Keanu made sure to deposit that exact amount into her bank account.

For one of his birthdays, he walked into a bakery, bought a brioche, had one single candle put into it, and celebrated his birthday with the locals by offering coffee to anyone who wanted to talk to him.

Another time when he was in Los Angeles, according to paparazzi who were following him, he befriended a homeless man and spent a few hours with him, sharing stories about their lives.

There is no doubt that if Keanu had not had the difficult upbringing that he had and the many tragedies, he would not have become such a warm-heated, compassionate, loving, giving person. Inside, he must have felt broken in many ways, but he didn't let that take him out of the game of life. Gratitude was the boat he floated on, which allowed him to sail on to better shores. This man could have done what most famous actors do, which usually has nothing to do with helping others. Instead, he chooses to get up and focus on the one thing that money cannot buy – the act of striving to be grateful and doing good deeds.

Isn't it rather interesting that those who have endured difficult times are the ones who are the most willing to help? The key is to not go down or stay down in any rabbit hole of negativity.

The Power Of Covenant Leadership

Now you understand that God is a self-sacrificing, non-violent, enemy loving God – and that He is Christ consciousness, self-sacrificial love epitomized at the cross. You now understand it was more than just Jesus dying on the cross for humanity; it was a reordering of the cosmos – a victory against Satan and his cohorts. And now, you can see that we are living in the aftermath of that.

When we fully comprehend God's love and then feel gratitude, we can then confidently, as God's viceroys, influence this world for the good. We are God's good seeds in this soil called earth. The aftermath meaning is very much like in WW II. The victory was won on D-Day, but there were still skirmishes going on for a while even though the war was over. We are fighting those skirmishes today against Satan even though the battle was won at the cross.

Today we need to produce leaders who can influence our world for the good. That takes biblical faith. The difference between biblical faith and the psychological faith that is common today is biblical faith is a covenant with God. When God's covenant partners voice the questions and objections to his appearance as strange and alien behavior, they are manifesting the confidence that the covenant relationship with God is solid enough to handle their expressions, complaints, confusion and even occasional accusation. And they are manifesting their confidence that, at the end of the day, God will demonstrate that he has the faithful and benevolent character he claims he has, appearances to the contrary notwithstanding. Whereas the modern psychology concepts motivate people to seek and cling to a feeling of certainty, the biblical concept is about retaining covenant trust in one's covenant partners in the face of uncertainty.

We can see covenantal leadership demonstrated in the life of Jesus Christ when we look at the humble, self-sacrificial character dramatically demonstrated at the cross. I have seen in many episodes of Jesus' life the temptations narrative, where Satan offered Jesus the authority of all the kingdoms on the earth, and all the splendor that came with that (Matt 4:8-10). Jesus came back to win back all those kingdoms, but he refused to bow down to Satan's coercive form of leadership. He instead came back to win these kingdoms with a self-sacrificial love of a cruciform life shown at the cross.

Also, Jesus taught his disciples about the misguided understanding of what The Messiah was going to look like. The Jewish nation was expecting a warrior king and yet Jesus came as a servant and to serve the people, giving his life up as a ransom for many.

Jesus continually taught his disciples that his life was heading towards Jerusalem to suffer and be executed. With this, Peter angrily tried to stop Jesus. Jesus turned around and told Peter he's a very good friend, but to *"get behind me Satan"* (Matt 16:23). This stern rebuke was because Jesus saw Satan's power working through Peter. Jesus was telling Peter his model of leadership was not the warrior king, but of the coercive nature of Satan. It was the antithesis of this demonstrated at the cross of a cruciform life. That was the model of leadership that Jesus was trying to teach the apostles and Satan was using Peter to resist that.

The point in the illustration happened when Jesus and his disciples celebrated the Passover meal. What do you do when you know that you have the power to do anything you want? Jesus put a towel around his waist and started to wash his disciples dusted, dirty feet even though these disciples would let Jesus down at his greatest hour of need. This is the humble, other orientated, Cruciform character that Jesus displayed throughout his cross centered ministry. This is the model of leadership that is vastly different from today's understanding of what leadership looks like.

In this chapter, we want to focus on the cruciform characteristics shown throughout history of God's people leaders, emulating the spirit and nature of a suffering servant, enemy loving, non-violent, other orientated model of leadership. This is the kind of leadership that the world desperately needs today.

BIBLICAL EXAMPLES OF COVENANT LEADERS

Noah: *Wrestled in keeping a clean mind (Gen 6:5).* At a time when God saw that every thought of a man was evil, except for Noah and his family, He decided to scrape his current creation and start over. Noah would not be influenced by man's wicked thinking; he held onto keeping his mind clean (John 10:10).

Jesus said that Satan came to steal, kill and destroy, but He came to give you life. Jesus said to recognize the voice of Satan. The fact that Noah's family was not part of his culture's thinking says a lot about his silent warfare with Satan. He saved his family with his fortitude. Covenant leaders take stock of their thinking. They understand that it is the craft that can fly above the enemy's line. They hear a lot of noise, being people's opinion, but they protect their mind to stay the course. Covenant leaders are amazing organizers because they go into their minds where the future lies and then stay the course.

Abraham: SELFLESS – Giving not selfish. Abraham gave up the comfort of his own home, culture and friends to follow the calling that God had on his life. This was a selfless act that not many people would do – travel to a different country, to a different people, into a different land. He brought along with him his nephew Lot. He brought along his herdsman and his sheep. As they were roaming their part of the world, the herds of sheep and men grew. But problems started to arise amongst the herdsmen. Abraham divided them and gave half to Lot. The fighting and problems continued until Abraham thought it would be better that Lot take his herd and herdsman and go in one direction and him and his herdsman go in another!

It was obvious to everyone that there were better pastures to choose from. In humility, Abraham allowed Lot to choose where he wanted to go. This was a selfless act of Abraham. Lot chose the greener pastures. Abraham accepted his choice, and they went about their life living. After a short period of time, Lot was badly influenced by his culture and Abraham remained steadfast in his selfless life. When Abraham heard how much trouble Lot was in, he selflessly came to help him and his family.

The point is that covenant leaders can put themselves second place to any situation that benefits the majority. They are selfless people.

Joseph: *Pure-hearted.* Joseph saw the good in everything even though his brothers were jealous. He had a dream that showed his entire family kneeling before him. When he told his family about the dream, his brothers got so jealous of his perceived arrogance that they sold him and put him in a pit. Next, they had to decide whether to kill him or sell him. They decided to sell him.

Regardless, Joseph still loved all the members of his family.

He was sold to Potiphar who quickly saw Joseph's character and integrity and entrusted him with the running of his whole household. However, Potiphar's wife took a liking to Joseph and tried to have sex with him. But Joseph said that her husband had entrusted him with everything and that there was no way that he would have a relationship with her. Regardless, she grabbed his cloak and he ran away. She then turned around and falsely accused him of trying to rape her. As a result of that, he was sent to prison.

In prison, he was really well-liked by all the jailers because he was helping people with problems they had and also by interpreting their dreams and circumstances. One of the prisoners was a cupbearer to Pharaoh. Joseph interpreted his dream and told him he would be restored as the cupbearer to Pharaoh. This gave the cupbearer hope for his freedom. This interpretation came true and the cupbearer was released from prison. Joseph appealed to him to help him to get out of prison. But the cupbearer forgot about Joseph for two years.

Pharaoh had dreams that nobody could interpret. That was when the cupbearer remembered Joseph. Joseph was then brought out of prison and interpreted the Pharaoh's dream so well that Pharaoh knew that Joseph was a man of great wisdom. He then made Joseph the second most powerful man in the world.

When Joseph's family finally came to Egypt because of severe famine, they unknowingly came right before Joseph's feet, therefore fulfilling his earlier dream. Joseph cried with joy when he saw his family and had no resentment. When Joseph finally revealed who he really was, his family was both shocked and in fear. They were fearful of him because they expected anybody who went through what they put him through to have resentment, anger, and bitterness. Regardless, Joseph chose not to be that in his heart.

Joseph, like Jesus, was pure-hearted and accepted his fate. He didn't allow poison to be in his heart. He was happy to serve. He accepted the power of a cruciform Heart. He allowed no bitterness in his heart. Covenant leaders understand how to handle insults, misjudgments, and negative, rude people. They know the space the negativity is coming from, so they know it's not personal – it's the work of Satan.

Covenant leaders faced many difficulties – many ups and downs, but they are people of pure-heartedness and tenacious perseverance.

Moses: *Trusted God's method, not his own.* Moses was raised a prince; he killed an Israelite and had to flee Egypt. He spent 40 years in the desert. Then Moses was asked by God to go back into Egypt as a shepherd, not a prince, with just a staff in his hand and to ask pharaoh to *"let my people go."*

At first Moses made excuses such as he couldn't talk, so God gave him Aaron his brother. As the story progresses, Aaron did little of the talking; it was mainly Moses. I believe the initial struggle that Moses had was to just trust God in looking weak and insignificant talking to pharaoh and saying to the most powerful man on the earth, *"let my people go."* This is like when Jesus appeared weak but freed us from sin.

Covenant leaders create trust around them because the people see how they trust God and people. They appear to look vulnerable, but the strength is not in them, but in God.

David: *A Healer of people.* David lived under the tyrannical leadership of Saul who was proud, insecure, and threatened by David because of his popularity with the people. Saul tried to kill David and drove him out of the land because he was jealous that people sang songs about his victories. David fled to the cave of Adullam. When he left, 400 men followed him. They were distressed or in debt or discontented (1 Sam 22:2), yet David accepted them, regardless of his own problems.

He created jobs for them as security for the farmers from the Philistines. He gave them a vision for themselves and their families. They became the mighty men of David. From the discontentment they felt, to the confident protectors of the land, he changed their whole life and their family's lives.

Covenant Leaders are resourceful; they want to help and heal people in all areas of life.

Solomon: *Trusted his gut.* King Solomon was faced with a challenge when two women brought one child to him and both declared that the child was theirs. Both women were very persuasive about them being the mother of the child. Solomon trusted his gut and said OK, cut the child in two with the sword and give each woman half. As the soldier was about to split the child in half, one of the women said no, let the other woman have the child. Then Solomon gave the child to the woman who stopped the soldier, declaring that this was the real mother.

Solomon was known all around the world for his wisdom. This was an act where he trusted his gut feeling about how to find the true mother. To trust your gut, you must know yourself and align yourself with your subconscious mind. Trusting your gut means putting your spiritual antennas up so that you are emotionally aware of your feelings. It's also about trusting that God speaks to you through them.

Covenant leaders have a good sense of how the gut feels and trust it. They make decisions based on that.

Peter: *Open book.* Whatever Peter was thinking, he would just say it. Whether he looked or felt stupid, he just let you know where he stood. He wasn't manipulative, he wasn't trying to be shrewd, he wasn't working his own agenda; he was just a real person who spoke openly about what he was thinking. There was never any doubt about who Peter was. Out of the 12 apostles, Jesus chose Peter to lead because with Peter, there was always full disclosure.

The first sermon after Jesus' resurrection in the book of Acts was given by Peter, declaring that Jesus was God, that Jesus was the Messiah and that everybody in that crowd was responsible for killing Jesus. His honesty, his openness and sincerity convicted over 3,000 people that day who were baptized into the name of Jesus Christ because they knew Peter could be trusted.

Covenant leaders have no selfish agenda, they are real, they are sincere, and they're open about their lives and their beliefs and plans. They radiate integrity that permeates trust. Our world is in desperate need of people like Peter.

Paul: *Change Agent.* Paul was called by God. He had one of the highest Pedigrees in the Jewish Synagogue order. He persecuted the church and saw Stephen get stoned to death. He wanted to change the impact the Christian movement was having on the Jewish world. But then he met Jesus and realized what he was doing was wrong! In a spirit of repentance, Paul was led blind into Damascus where he fasted for three days out of remorse for the cruelty he showed to the Christians. Then he got up and got baptized. The change agent was born.

He caused so much havoc for correcting the Jews in Damascus that they had to lower him down at night in a basket to escape from being killed. Paul didn't let his religiosity limit him.

He changed. He fervently explained Jesus accurately as the true Messiah which the Jews rejected and persecuted Paul because of it.

Then he was called into the Gentile World to change their understanding of God. Peter came and visited Paul and saw how he broke from the Jewish traditions and enjoyed the freedom of God with a gentile world. When James and John came down from Jerusalem, Peter pulled away and started reverting back to his Jewish practices. Paul challenged Peter in front of James and John to change. Paul walked in to all cultural and religious environments to teach and change people's perspective of God and Jesus.

In addition, Paul wrote letters to teach communities to change and have a godly perspective towards their community. He wanted to talk to all leaders to the highest level which is why he ended up in Rome to try and talk to Caesar.

Paul was called by God to be a change agent. Covenant leaders understand they are called. They understand there is a sacred side to their life. They feel the need to change family, culture, and community and try to influence the world to be a better place.

God needs more change agents in our culture. Do you feel the pull from God in your life to be a change agent?

THE INFLUENCE OF COVENANT LEADERSHIP

The gladiatorial games were merciless, bloodthirsty entertainment for Roman citizen fans who watched as Christians were fed to the lions including entire families with children. These surrendered Christians suffered unthinkable horrors. But these gladiatorial games mysteriously just stopped happening. The theory is that the merciless killings eventually convicted the conscience of sincere Romans. They began to disdain the games. Christians who were willing to surrender their lives voluntarily stopped the most tyrannical government that has ever existed in the world.

This is a point on its own – the power of surrendered leadership – they surrendered their lives to the glory of God.

Because of their cruciform, Christ-like, cross-like nature, they influenced the most blood-thirsty nation in the world – Rome. There was no fight. They relied solely on prayer.

One of my concerns with the Christendom world today is there are no men and women aspiring to be major influences in our society. Many of the preachers haven't figured out how to be more progressive. They are too trapped in the religiosity system. My calling is to get them out of the system and help them train to be influencers in society.

MY PERSONAL EXPERIENCE IN INFLUENCING

A big part of leadership is influencing others. As I mentioned before, when I was an evangelist in the city of London England, I had the opportunity to meet Marcus Gayle. He was like an NBA basketball star or an NFL player to the Europeans. He played against the likes of David Beckham. I wanted to influence the community of

London, so I started playing soccer with Marcus on Thursday evenings in a place called Shepherds Bush...

Marcus started to bring along some semi-professional players and eventually the community started to come out and watch our games. Soon after, very good teams started bartering to play us on Thursday evenings. I then went to meet with an established club in West London Place called Hanwell. I wanted to be the second team and amalgamated our team with their team. I knew, with time, we would become the main team.

From there I thought we could become a professional team because of the talent and the unity that we could forge as Christians. It was all starting to unfold in an amazing way but then I got called to serve in another part of the world.

The experience opened my eyes to see that Christians with a vision and conviction could really influence society.

WHAT ARE THE QUALITIES OF A GREAT LEADER?

Covenant leaders are effective and dynamic. They feel a sense of calling and there is a sacred side to them. They understand that they are in touch with God, and they know that their calling is bigger than who they are – that's the quality of a leader.

In addition, they are passionate about what they believe in, not to impress people, but because they truly believe. They feel it – they get excited about their passions. This is why great leaders must be authentic.

A covenant leader doesn't mind making mistakes or hitting any walls because of the strong faith in God that they have that everything is going to work out one way or another. Also, great leaders feel a passion that bubbles over to others. Their strong belief and convictions are felt by others and they can easily motivate and inspire others to their vision.

Covenant leaders are also well organized – they know what they are trying to do. They are focused on their vision and how to get there. Also, they do not feel threatened by anyone because they know that there is nothing to fear when God is on their side. Furthermore, they are secure in who they are and don't mind the opinions of others. They understand that *"with much counsel, victory is assured,"* as the scripture puts it. This is why a great leader values the thoughts, feelings and input from others.

But also, a covenant leader sees themselves as a servant, just as Jesus demonstrated when he washed the feet of the apostles. Leaders are willing to work long hours. They also continually learn new things and are always growing – always trying to develop themselves. The result is a feeling of confidence and poise, even under very stressful situations.

A covenant leader also has a vivid imagination. They can clearly see the future where others cannot. They can see the long-term view of things and think in terms of the future instead of short-term gratification and payoff.

They are also able to summarize matters and make hard decisions quickly. And they can persevere and make decisive decisions that they stick to.

Covenant leaders are also charismatic. Their moral values and integrity give them a certain charming personality which, to most, is endearing. They make every person that they talk to feel important because they value everyone equally.

At the same time, they are humble and will praise others in a heartbeat even when they had a big part in their success.

WE NEED MORE COVENANT LEADERS

I believe one of the things that is hurting our country and the world is the lack of leadership. Christians don't aspire enough to be an influence in the seven mountains of society. It all starts from being the best of what you're doing currently and allowing God to lead you to places you never thought you could get to but most are not encouraged in our Christian world to be our very best.

There is not enough teaching about excelling. Instead, mediocrity and religiosity are more warmly regarded. But we need to be in the marketplace every day of the week instead of just once a week. We have lost our sight, our vision, and our goals in favor of a meager presence in society.

Many Christians will go to church regularly on Sunday and then forget who they really are Monday through

Saturday. And they may abstain from sinful behavior but never declare that they "want to be a leader."

But the world needs more disciples of Christ to be covenant leaders...

CHAPTER 8: BORN TO BE ALIVE

You were born to be alive in every sense of the word. When I say "alive," I mean enjoying life to the fullest because you've put your trust in God, have a solid foundation because of that relationship, and can then become your best, powerful, co-creative self. Most of us live lives of quiet desperation, without any real help or guidance on how to change anything. And most self-help books don't include God into the picture, which makes their path much more difficult.

But it is my belief that if you can trust in God and if you understand that you are a co-creator with him on earth, then your life can be filled with meaning, success, and abundance in all aspects of life, not just a couple.

We all need help. So many programs will charge you $1,000 to improve your financial situation without any guarantee for success. The problem is, they only address one aspect – money. But what about all the other areas? What about family? What about health? What about community? What about your spiritual side? When only one aspect is addressed, the wheel of life becomes very lop-sided and then you cannot smoothly move forward. This is why I believe that you must seek to improve all areas in terms of setting goals and doing all you can to be the best version of yourself.

The Christian Church needs to get more up-to-speed with the times in regard to self-help and personal development. They need to be more proactive with assisting their followers to excel in life, to strive to be better, to do more for themselves and others, to be the leaders of the free world, and to be spiritually and financially free.

Nowadays, there are a lot of beneficial, scientifically proven systems, tools and techniques that can be used to create the spiritually and financially free life that we all desire. I believe that God wants us to use all our faculties and all of the tools available to us. God does not want you to lead a mediocre life. And He said at Matthew 19:26, that "with God, all things are possible." God wants you to lead a happy, secure, joyful, abundant life.

So, if there are tools out there that can be used to help us, then why not use them? Why shy away from it simply because it's not in the Bible? If we decided that no new tools should be used because it's not in the Bible, then no Christian should use the Internet because it's not in the Bible either.

But what are these tools that are available, and how can you use them to help?

HOW TO REMOVE LIMITING BELIEFS

One of the biggest problems that I see people have in improving their life is that they have limiting beliefs that hold them back. It's as if they were programmed to have only a certain amount of success, and nothing more. But what they usually can't see is that the problem is within them – it's what they think and believe about themselves that stops them from living their best life – nothing more.

There is a good chance that you too might fall into that category, and I would really like to help you to get out of the trap of limiting beliefs. Fortunately, there are new ways to do that, and I want to briefly introduce you to a couple of them that I think will really help you to remove any blocks to success that you may have.

Don't feel bad if you have limiting beliefs. Most people have them. Most people have been programmed to lead a life of mediocrity instead of excellence. But what I want for you is to let go of your old beliefs. Let go of the past mistakes and regrets. Let go of any negative thought that you are not good enough, not smart enough, too young, too old, too whatever. Excuses be gone, as the late Dr. Dyer used to say. Don't let excuses rule your life. Decide right now that your main goal is to become a more positive person. See yourself as the type of person who looks at the glass as half full instead of half empty. Be the type of person who you admire.

You may be thinking, "I've tried this before. I can't seem to get past my negative thinking and beliefs. Even when I want to, I can't stop it. I feel doomed!" If you feel this way, don't worry. There are new tools that you can use that can really help, and I will introduce you to two of them here.

In order to change your personal reality, you have to change your personality. You must become the person who you want to be before you see any external difference. You have to find a way to start believing in yourself again. You must get back to the person who you really are, and not allow the words from others or the events from the past determine and define who you are.

You are nothing less than a magnificent being who was born onto planet earth to experience joy, happiness, success, abundance, growth and expansion. If you are reading this, you are worthy. If you have made it this far, you have what it takes to be your best. It's simply a matter of deciding if you really want it, or not. But I get the feeling that you want it.

The personal development and self-help genre have many solutions on how to remove limiting beliefs. New science has shown us that people really can remove their limiting beliefs to excel in every manner of life that they want.

The beliefs that you hold about yourself and your world has a drastic effect on your life experience. For example, if you believe that you aren't good enough for some reason, then your subconscious mind will do all that it can possibly do in order to keep that reality true. It will sabotage you without you even knowing it. Goals will be extremely hard if not impossible to obtain if you don't believe that you can succeed, or that you don't deserve it.

This is where relatively new tools in the self-help and personal development genre come in handy. One of these methods is called Neuro Linguistic Programming or NLP for short.

NEURO-LINGUISTIC PROGRAMMING AND GOAL SETTING

Neuro-Linguistic Programming, or NLP, is a set of tools that were created to take control of your own thinking – to re-program your subconscious mind. The main way that they created it was by modeling successful people by analyzing their thoughts, feelings, emotions, and even bodily movements. Tony Robbins, famous self-help guru, talks a lot about how when you are depressed, your shoulders hunch over, you look to the ground, and your whole body gives in to the effects of gravity. But when you simply sit up straight and hold your head up high, you can't get depressed. Try it the next time you feel down!

NLP is a lot more than just body position, however. It uses practical techniques to relieve the emotional charge to past events and instead, "program" into the subconscious mind much better, healthier, supportive perspectives and beliefs.

It was created by co-founder Richard Bandler, who was disappointed with traditional psychotherapy. He partnered up with Virginia Satir who was well-known as the "mother of family therapy." They put their heads together and came up with NLP.

NLP provides practical ways in which you can change the way that you think, view past events, and approach your life.

According to NLP, when you set a goal, you should focus on what you want to have instead of what you don't. It's a little like the concept of the Law of Attraction where you get what you focus on. For example, if you want to lose weight, it's better to make your goal to "be fit and trim" rather than focus on the negative goal of to "lose the fat."

NLP also believes that your mind is always trying to find answers to questions that you ask it. But you must not ask negative questions like "Why do I feel so bad?" because your subconscious mind will work overtime in the background, finding all kinds of reasons why you feel bad, therefore making you feel even worse.

You should stick to more positive questions like, "How will I feel when I change for the better?" Or "What can I do in order to feel better about myself?"

Just a slightly more positive positioning of questions can make all the difference in the world as to whether you are able to create a supportive goal, or a detrimental one.

NLP relies on visualization to affect how you feel. For example, one thing NLP would have a person do is to remove negative feelings about someone who is a problem to you by imagining that they are put into a small box and moved far away from you. The positive side to this would be to think of someone who you really like and make the image of them bigger and bigger and observe how much better you feel.

There is a lot to NLP and it's too involved to get into all of it here. But there is another energy healing, self-improvement tool that a lot of NLP practitioners think may be even better – it's called, "The Emotional Freedom Technique."

EMOTIONAL FREEDOM TECHNIQUES

Another amazingly effective way to help yourself to remove limiting beliefs and the fear of failure is a technique called "Emotional Freedom Techniques," otherwise known as EFT. EFT was created by a man named Gary Craig who was trained by PhD psychologist, Dr. Roger Callahan.

When you understand Dr. Callahan's story, you'll start to understand the power of EFT and its many uses.

Dr. Callahan was a western taught Doctor of Psychology. He was working with a client who had an inordinate fear of water. She was so fearful of water, that she got extreme anxiety simply washing her face, or standing near a body of water like the ocean, a pool, or a river.

Callahan worked with his client using every westernized method he could for a solid two years and gained little progress. Frustrated and nearly at his wits end, he decided to look at eastern medicine for solutions. This meant studying things such as acupressure points on the body and learning about something called energy meridians that are supposed to run from the acupressure points to parts of the brain.

He understood that touching and holding acupressure points could alleviate physical pain. But what about fear and emotional pain? Could it be possible? Could it help his client's fear of water?

The next time that he saw his female client with the fear of water, he asked her if she would like to try an experiment. She agreed.

He asked his client to think about her fear of water and to repeat her fear out loud while tapping on several different energy meridian endpoints on her body...

Very surprisingly to both, after just one round of tapping, his female client jumped out of her seat, declared that she was cured, ran over to the nearby restroom where the sink was, and started splashing water all over her face...

Next, she ran down to the community pool that was in the complex and got so close to the edge of it that Dr. Callahan had to ask her to please be careful to not fall in!

His client was instantly cured of her fear of water...

Two years of traditional therapy, versus 10 minutes...

Dr. Callahan devised an elaborate, complex tapping system called Thought Field Therapy (TFT) and he charged a lot of money for people to learn it. Gary Craig was one of his students.

But Gary, with permission from Dr. Callahan, took what Dr. Callahan had created, simplified it, and gave a free 85-page eBook to anyone who wanted to learn the basics. And that is how EFT, or Emotional Freedom Techniques was born...

EFT is an amazing tool that can be used to relieve physical and emotional pain like no other energy healing tool on the planet. Today, there are many proponents of EFT, including the late Dr. Wayne Dyer, Dr. Bruce Lipton, Dr. Dawson Church, self-help guru Bob Proctor and others.

No one knows exactly why and how it works, but regardless, millions of people have used it worldwide with incredible results. It has even been approved by the American Medical Association and the VA to be used for PTSD. Gary Craig, the creator of EFT, healed many vets on camera – and these were guys who had endured unbelievable events of human tragedy. Most of them couldn't ever get a good night sleep because of vivid nightmares. But with every single veteran that Gary worked with, EFT healed them.

EFT can be used for a wide variety of physical and emotional problems such as back pain, stress, fears, anxiety, and more. It can even be used for sports performance enhancement, public speaking, test taking, and phobias such as the fear of heights, the fear of flying, claustrophobia, panic attacks, heart palpitations and more.

But how can you use EFT for getting rid of limiting beliefs and the fear of failure?

A limiting belief gets created from conclusions that our subconscious mind makes after experiencing a certain event. For example, if you were put on the spot when you were only 8 years old to speak in front of the classroom and you weren't prepared, and you did poorly, your subconscious mind would create a belief that you're not a good speaker. And if you have another similar event happen like that which didn't go well either, then your subconscious mind reaffirms the strength of the belief and basically says, "See there? I told you that you weren't a good speaker!"

This belief can cause you to have an unfounded fear when it comes to public speaking, no matter how prepared you may be. And limiting beliefs can have other, side-bar negative beliefs that support one another in a sort of hierarchy of detailed events and the consequential negative belief. For example, if you also have the belief that you aren't smart enough, the public speaking belief and the "you aren't smart enough" belief work hand in hand together in order to keep that limiting belief alive and well.

But with a tool like EFT, you address those past negative events when you were a child and literally remove the emotional pain and intensity down to a 0 out of a possible 10. And when you do that, you free yourself from the emotional pain, thereby freeing you up to be your real, true, authentic self.

With EFT, you can remove the heart-felt negative pain from every event you've ever had, no matter how severe it might have been. And when you do get to that place of "emotional freedom," a whole new world can open to you. No longer will you sabotage your efforts or hold yourself back. You can be the confident person who you really are deep down and go for your dreams with a new elevated energy and passion that you haven't had before.

As far as the fear of failure is concerned, to remove it, the process is the same. Identify the times in your past when you failed and it felt really bad and tap for it. Most of us hold on to the fear of failing because of the emotional pain that we had as children when we first failed. But when you can tap away that fear, and any current fear of failure, you'll find that it is much easier to attempt to reach your goals in life, no matter how big or small.

That's the beauty of the EFT tool – you can quite literally delete the negative programming that you may have and re-write the program with positive, uplifting thoughts, feelings and beliefs about yourself.

Many NLP practitioners mainly use EFT because it seems to be more effective. If you want to learn more about NLP and EFT, please go to www.borntobealive.info. We do workshops on both of these tools and it will be very valuable to you.

A Practical Tool to Help You

Now that you understand the concepts of how to be spiritually and financially free, it is time to put it into practice. To help myself and others, I have created a workbook which includes information on how to set goals and a month 1 to month 12 calendar that you can start using any time of the year. This workbook is a conglomeration of the best things I know in regard to accomplishing your goals in the most effective possible.

Basically, there are 6 probing steps that you will go through namely,

How to Set Goals

Year in Review

Start in Gratitude

Guidelines

The Design

Why and How to Work on YOU First

In this workbook, you will learn more about "The Wheel of Life" which covers 8 important aspects of life in which to set your goals. Most people think of goal setting in one or two areas such as money and health. But there is so much more to your life than just that. And if all you focus on is your money and your health, other areas that will likely be important to you too, like family, will suffer. The key to leading a happy and fulfilled life is to be balanced in all 8 areas of life – not just a couple.

From the wheel of life, the workbook will ask you questions to clearly understand what your reasons are for having the goal, help you to understand your "why" so that you will stay motivated and inspired, and then explain the real reason why accomplishing any big goal is so important (it's probably not what you think!). In addition, it will help you to break down goals into meaningful, easy steps.

It also has a section to review the last year so that you can feel good about what you have already accomplished and get inspired to do more. I call it, "plan, do and review." For example, part of it will get you to list 10 great happenings from last year, and 10 lessons you learned. The workbook has space in it for you to write all your answers to all the questions. There are many pondering questions such as, "What are the three things I want to stop doing next year?" The point is to help you to define the right goals for you for the next year, and then use the calendar to help you plan for and keep on track towards your goals.

You may have heard of the acronym "SMART" which is used to help people achieve their goals by George T. Doran and Peter Drucker. I use this to help you to make your goals **S**pecific, Manageable, **A**chievable, **R**ealistic and **T**ime sensitive which you can use in the workbook.

I recommend that you get a family member or a friend to help you create your SMART goals so that you can get healthy feedback from them.

Final Word

I hope you have found this book to be a valuable tool and asset to see that when you have a strong, spiritual relationship with God, then everything can be added to you from there. "With God, all things are possible," says the scripture. And when you have that strong foundation, it makes it much easier for you to use the latest self-help tools to have the abundant life that you want.

The world is in desperate need of great leaders of integrity – what I like to call, Covenant Leaders – leaders who are not afraid to stand up for what is right, to take the lead in commerce and even in politics and help the world through their efforts guided by Christ Consciousness. That to me is the most important aspect of this book – helping to inspire spiritually strong leaders for the sake of all humanity.

But regardless of whether you become a Covenant leader, my wish and hope for you is that you gain valua ble insight on how to lead a happy life – one that is filled with joy, happiness, contentment and purpose. When your actions are in alignment with Christ consciousness 24/7 instead of just one day a week, you will improve YOU – and by improving yourself, every area of your life will be better.

Thank you for trusting in me with your valuable time. I give you my best wishes for a successful future.

If you want to know more, I do offer the daily/weekly/monthly planner workbook "Born to Be Alive" which will help you to put all this information to practical use. You can find that at www.borntobealive.info if you are interested.

May God bless you in every possible manner...